Book One: The /

Book One: The Adventures of Ichi and His Friends

presents

& His Friends!

BOOK ONE
The Journey to Mountain Temple

Book One: The Adventures of Ichi and His Friends

THE ADVENTURES OF

& His Friends!

BOOK ONE
The Journey to Mountain Temple

Characters and story
created and written by
Michael Matsuda

Characters drawn by
Michael Matsuda &
Eleazar Del Rosario

Book One: The Adventures of Ichi and His Friends

Dedication

To my little boy Sparky, who
brought so much joy into my life.
To my wife Karen, who never
stopped supporting my dream.

Book One: The Adventures of Ichi and His Friends

Acknowledgements

To my Lord Jesus, with Him,
all things are possible.
To the creativity of Mario Prado
and the encouragement of Art Camacho.
To the Shaw Brothers, who were my inspiration.
To Alexander Fu Sheng, Buck Sam Kong,
Lyle Fujioka and Cecil Peoples, my
martial arts influence.
To Fariborz Azhakh, the man who
made it all possible.
To Bryan Konietzko and Michael
Dante DiMartino for lighting the flame.
To my mom. When I was just a few years
old, she saw a spark of creativity in my eyes.
To Elaezar Del Rosario, for adding
his artistic genius to my characters and
making them magically come alive.
Finally, to all those wonderful people who
gave of themselves, their time,
their finances and their hopes,
who made the museum come true.

Table of Contents

Table of Contents

Book One: The Adventures of Ichi and His Friends

Introduction
Michael Matsuda, author/creator

When I was a very young man, just a teenager in the 1970s, I was able to get a job as a graphic artist for Walt Disney Productions. Back then, there were no computers, just a typewriter and hand drawings. I really enjoyed the style in which Disney used to promote their characters and how each of them played a huge role in Walt Disney's vision.

So, that's what I wanted to do here. As founder and president of the Martial Arts History Museum, I wanted to add that special touch that would make the museum in a sort, mirror the incredible success of Disneyland and the Disney Company. I loved how Disneyland, after over 50 years old, was still able to connect with both the young and old.

Like Mickey Mouse, Donald Duck, Pluto, and so many more characters became not only a product but a child's connection to Disneyland. I wanted a group of characters that young people would be able to connect to the museum as well.

I first began in the year 2000 by creating a fun dragon. It didn't turn out well. It looked more like an alligator. It wasn't until around ten years later that I came out with my first, great character, Sifu. Because I love Chinese kung fu and watched all those Shaw Bros. kung fu movies, there was always a teacher figure in nearly every movie.

Starting my career as a graphic artist, I know what works well together, how to blend things, how to create covers, write copy, I know add creativity to an otherwise boring design. Although I am also an artist because graphic design work does require some artwork, I can draw anything that's needed. However, I am a very slow artist. What takes my brother-in-law, Paul Wee, who is the head animator for *The Simpsons*, just a few hours to do, takes me six months to do.

My first character, Sifu.

Anyway, the Sifu character has been used over and over again in kung fu movies and by many different names, but they all share the same features; a teacher with a white beard, long white eyebrows and very full head of white hair.

To add that special connection to the television *Kung Fu* series, which I loved, I thought it would be nice to have Sifu hold out a pebble so that the student could grab, just like in the show.

I first opened my trusty photoshop program and drew my Sifu character. However, it was pretty dull, so I needed to add that special "Disney touch." So, I was introduced to Eleazar Del Rosario, a very talented artist, and I turned by drawing over to him. He put his very special, artistic talent to work and out popped precisely what I envisioned in my head. It was beautiful!

That's it! I said. That's the "Disney style" I was looking for.

As I did a photoshop design for each character, I sent them off to Eleazar and he made them come alive.

My vision of making characters to connect to the museum was a success and that, is how the characters were born.

The story you are about to read was completely created in my mind. Although I write a book every year, I'm ashamed to say that I'm not an avid reader. I have only read one children's book in my entire adult life and it was a Halloween book.

What I'm trying to say is that this entire story is completely mine. I did not use anyone else's story nor anyone else's idea.

Book One: The Adventures of Ichi and His Friends

The Adventure Begins

The evening was almost here and in just moments, the glowing warmth of the sun would gently close its eyes and make room for the night sky to awaken. You could feel a cool and welcoming breeze as the leaves from the garden began their dance around the hallways of Mountain Temple.

The night sky had unveiled it's dark beauty as millions upon millions of shining stars continued to illuminate the heavens, each one appearing brighter than the one before. The stars became so radiant that it felt like you could reach out your hand, grab one and stuff it into your pocket.

Off in the distance, you could hear the sound of a large bell being struck three times. "GONG! GONG! GONG!" the sound rumbled and echoed throughout the temple, signaling suppertime for the monks.

Our group gathered at the Northern-most dining area. There were five of us in all. This included Sifu, who was assigned as our teacher.

The eating arrangements, one had to admit, were a little peculiar to say the least!

The structure in which our particular group gathered was surrounded by only three walls and a roof. The fourth wall was actually no wall at all! In fact, it was completely open to the elements. Sifu said that the fourth wall served to remind us to be one with the Earth and to welcome the natural world into our midst.

Suppertime was a very special time at Mountain Temple. It was not only a time to gather, relax, unwind and for everyone to fill their bellies after a hard day's work, but it gave everyone an opportunity to work together as a team in order to prepare the evening's feast.

One of the children gathered the wood for the fire. Another prepared the table and two of them cooked the meal. When everyone was finished eating, they all joined together to clear the table and wash the dishes.

Every day brought a different task for the children. However, everyone loved it when Sifu prepared the dessert! It was a family recipe that had never been changed. It was so delicious it was like eating a piece of heaven! Yummm!

The Great Tree

The history of Mountain Temple can be traced back over two thousand years.

In fact, it has been said that the table in which we ate upon was one of the oldest and most scared pieces of the temple!

According to Sifu, this very table had been part of the oldest tree known to man.

"For centuries, the 'Great Tree' was a big part of the community. In the summertime, it gave the people shade and in the wintertime, it gave them protection from the snow. It bore fruit to give the people food and it blossomed with the most beautiful flowers you had ever seen! It weathered the fiercest storms and the driest droughts. The great tree gave them hope and encouragement."

"But alas," he concluded, "tragedy struck the Great Tree."

"What happened to it, Sifu?" asked Kekoa, with a puzzled look on her face as she placed both hands on the table in anticipation of an answer to her question.

"One day, there was the storm of storms and bolts of lightning were striking across the entire village," Sifu motioned as he continued, "and it was damaging everything in sight!"

"Anything and everything was catching fire! It seemed like the entire village was doomed!"

Sifu paused for moment and then continued.

"Then somehow, as if by magic - as if the Great Tree realized the tragedy that was happening to the village - it somehow, someway made itself into a lightning rod! Every bolt of lightning thereafter directed itself at the Great Tree. The lightning continued to hit the Great Tree so furiously and with such force it caused the ground to tremble! As it would during an earthquake!

Eventually, the multitude of strikes broke the

Great Tree into a thousand pieces!"

Sifu continued, "When the storm ended, the village was saved, but all were saddened to learn that the Great Tree was destroyed. Together, the elders decided to create a way to keep the memory of the Great Tree alive so that everyone could appreciate how it sacrificed itself to save the village."

"Quickly, the villagers gathered the best craftsmen and woodworkers in the land. They decided that the best way to remember the Great Tree was to create a series of tables with the salvageable pieces. One of those tables," as Sifu looked down, "is right here before us."

"Really? For reals?" exclaimed Lalo with the look of excitement in his eyes.

"Woowww! How neat is that!" exclaimed Kekoa.

"Yes, really. This is an actual part of the Great Tree," said Sifu, smiling as he said so and with great pride.

"Wow, that's a very cool story Sifu," commented Ichi.

The table before them was about six inches thick. Although it had been properly prepared and glazed over, you could still see a multitude of nicks, cuts and scratches from hundreds of years of use.

"Tonight is our very first, official meal together," Sifu stood up, adjusted his robe a bit and said, "Being able to eat at this table is one of the great privileges and we should always show our respect. We not only celebrate the life of this Great Tree from which it came, but we also celebrate the thousands upon thousands of brave warriors that sat at this very table and dined."

"No way," replied Shinji as he looked at his reflection in the table.

"Yes way," said Sifu. "It was here that some of the greatest warriors would gather and share stories of fierce battles, friendships and good deeds. Eating together was a time of rejoicing. It was a time of brotherhood and sisterhood, it was a time in which everyone could gather and speak their mind and pass on the wisdom of many generations."

"And stuff their bellies too," laughed Lalo.

"Right," as Sifu patted his belly, "I have had much practice."

Everyone started laughing.

The dining table was purposely set low to the ground. Instead of chairs, there were six over-sized pillows; A yellow one for Lalo, a blueish one for Kekoa, a green one for Shinji, a beige one for Ichi and Sifu needed two red ones, in order to be more comfortable.

Unfortunately, the old sitting pillows were in much need of love and care.

The feathers and stuffing that provided their bounciness and comfort, were nearly flat. The wear and tear of everyone's fannies over the years had obviously taken their toll.

Shinji would often need to fluff up his pillow at least five times before he was comfortable. From squeezing them to punching them, he was never satisfied. Everyone had to suffer for two whole weeks until they found a new set of pillows that everyone could enjoy.

The Suppertime Challenge

Sifu's favorite time of the day and favorite meal of the day was suppertime.

Just as the food was about to hit the table he would always say, "Ahh, I know this is going to be the best meal ever," as he stroked his long white goatee at least three times, "Yes, I have a feeling this will be very delicious."

Although each had their turn at setting the table, everyone loved it when it was Lalo's turn. As the son of a King, Lalo had been used to the finer things in life.

However, despite being royalty, Lalo's parents insisted that he learn how to do the duties of the servants, which included learning how to set an elegant table. So, when it was Lalo's turn at Mountain Temple, the table settings were magnificent and even included napkin swans. For some reason, it made the dinner taste a little better.

Since Kekoa and Ichi were the eldest of the group, Sifu insisted they cook the very first meal. Mmmm! Mmmm! You could smell the beautiful aroma as they prepared the various, tasty dishes. The feast included noodles, rice, chicken, dumplings and steamed vegetables.

Since each of the kids were from different villages, Sifu insisted that they all got a chance to cook some of their own special traditional foods unique to each of their cultures.

Sifu believed that artistry is an expression of one's self and as such, it should be included in everything. In this case, it was in the presentation of all their meals.

Now, although most of the nearby villages ate with

forks and knives, Sifu insisted that all the students eat in the traditional way. This meant that everyone had to use chopsticks, which was fine with Ichi and Shinji because their families always ate with chopsticks!

Kekoa had the toughest time learning how to use chopsticks but Lalo caught on quickly. In just two days, Lalo was able to pick up a single grain of rice.

Although Sifu thoroughly enjoyed every one of his meals, and especially the deserts, he did have a fondness for a good cup of tea.

He enjoyed every flavor he could find. From raspberry teas to cherry teas to even vanilla tasting teas, Sifu would consume each cup with great joy. He was always on the hunt for new flavors of tea.

Sifu believed that a good cup of tea should warm your day and soothe your night.

"Tonight," said Sifu, as he unfolded his legs and stood up again, "We are about to enjoy a fine meal. Please stand with me as we lift our cups and make our first of many toasts," expressed Sifu. "To family," everyone said in unison as they clinked their teacups together.

"Now, this looks scrumptious," said Sifu as he sat down and rubbed his tummy, then stroked his white beard at least three times.

This was everyone's first meal together, so the gang was willing to do anything they could to please Sifu.

"Check out these dumplings Sifu! Try it!" Ichi said as he quickly grabbed three dumplings and put them on Sifu's plate. "Oh, thank you," Sifu replied.

Just as Sifu was about to open his mouth and eat a dumpling, Kekoa said, "Wait Sifu! Try the roasted chicken! I cooked it for the belly of a warrior!"

"Well in that case, alright," Sifu responded humorously, as he smiled back at Kekoa, while grabbing a few pieces of chicken.

Less than a second later, Shinji literally tossed a bunch of noodles on Sifu's plate and said, "Sifu! Sifu! Try these noodles! They are delicious, yes?"

"Well I'll tell you in a just a moment," replied Sifu as he again tried to put some food in his mouth.

"Sifu, this is a very special rice that I know you will enjoy," pointed out Lalo, while placing a scoop on his plate. By this time, Sifu's plate was so filled with food that it looked like Mountain Temple itself!

With great anticipation, everyone looked at Sifu to see which dish he would try first. Sifu took his chopsticks and awkwardly, but successfully, picked up a noodle, a piece of rice, a dumpling and a piece of chicken all at the same time. He smiled broadly as he placed the delectable combination in his mouth.

"Now, that's how it's done!" said Sifu, as everyone laughed. Then, they all started eating with great gusto.

Say When!

Throughout the evening, everyone shared their stories about their journey to Mountain Temple. Although their adventures were carefully planned by Sifu, he was still thrilled to hear of their exploits and the interesting people they met along the way.

Toward the end of the meal, which would become a daily tradition, Sifu would do one of two things. He would either tell stories of the ancient days or enlighten the group with an insightful lesson.

He then stood up and patted his now full tummy. "My compliments to the chefs, Kekoa and Ichi, and the preparers, Lalo and Shinji. Let's once again, lift our cups to give thanks," Sifu said, as they all stood up and clinked their cups together. "Here, here!" they all replied.

"Now, allow me to fill your cups again. But this time, with some of my special tea!"

Gathering all the cups together, Sifu went into his pouch and took out a small package of herbs and emptied it into the teapot.

Grabbing the handle of the teapot in his right hand, Sifu lifted the pot as high as he could reach and poured the hot tea like a waterfall into each of the cups.

"We can learn about so many of life's lessons in many everyday things that we take for granted," explained Sifu as he looked toward the ceiling, still pouring the tea perfectly into each cup. "As an example, tomorrow the sun will come out and with its warm rays of sunshine, it greets us and welcomes in a new day."

"Yeah, it hits my eyes every morning and wakes me whether I like it or not!" Shinji jokingly said.

"Shinji, shhhhh! Listen to Sifu!" Ichi leaned over and whispered to Shinji.

Sifu continued, "Like right now, it is the cool breeze at night that blankets us with sleep and this tea, an old recipe passed down to me from my ancestors and made from nature itself, is a delicious way to enjoy our meals."

"Sifu, you are making me really thirsty!" said Lalo as he leaned forward with anticipation.

"Patience, Lalo," said Sifu as he motioned his hand like a fan encouraging the aroma to head in the kid's direction. "Can't you just smell that wonderful tea?"

"Hmmm. It smells like orange and vanilla," revealed Shinji. "Oranilla!"

"Shhhhh," whispered Kekoa. Shinji giggled as he lightly elbowed Lalo.

"As I pour our tea, there is a valuable lesson we can also learn from these simple cups," affirmed Sifu. By this time the third cup had already been filled. "Oh yes, and don't forget to say when," mentioned Sifu as he continued to pour the hot tea into the other two cups.

Finally, the tea reached the brim of the cup and began to overflow onto the table.

"Sifu!" Kekoa said, "I believe the cups are overflowing! You can stop, Sifu!"

Shinji turned to Kekoa and reminded her, "Sifu said you have to say when."

"Oh," Kekoa said with a smile like she was the only one who knew the secret password, "Then when."

But Sifu continued to pour the tea despite the many requests to stop!

"Yeah! When, Sifu! When!" shouted out Ichi as the tea continued to flow onto the table.

Despite the mess, Sifu continued to pour and said, "We must open our minds to new things."

Because of the mess Sifu was making, Shinji and Lalo laughed so hard, they fell off their pillows as Sifu finally stopped pouring and explained, "As you can see, these cups are too full, you can't pour any more into them."

"Please, allow me to explain," pointed out Sifu.

"Let this cup represent our life. We fill the cup with many wonderful things. We fill it with our experiences, we fill it with learning, we fill it with growing," as Sifu holds up the cup.

"When new ideas come, we can either be open to them, which means we empty our cup so that there is room for these new ideas."

Sifu then took one of the cups and lifted it up to his mouth. He then took a big sniff like he was about to inhale the entire cup of tea, blew on it for just a few moments and then drank the entire contents all at once.

"Aaaah!" Sifu exclaimed, as he wiped his mouth with his sleeve. "Now that..." remarked Sifu gleefully, "... was delicious," as he showed everyone an empty cup.

All the kids looked at Sifu with their mouths wide open.

"As you can see, my cup is now empty," as he pours in more tea. "Alas, new ideas are now pouring in."

"Or.... we keep our cup full, we don't even consider the new ideas, the new concepts, and thus, the cup overflows and all those new ideas run down onto the table," added Sifu, "as you witnessed earlier."

"So, we can either be open, which is an empty cup ready to be filled, or block them by being close minded, which is a full cup with no room for more tea. Does everyone understand?" said Sifu.

Lalo and Shinji each grabbed a cup. They put their noses close to the tea, smelled it intensely and gave it a few blows to cool it down. Like Sifu, they both drank it down and in unison exclaimed, "Aaaah!"

"Sifu," asked Ichi with a puzzled look on his face, "Does that mean we are supposed to forget all we have learned?"

"Just the opposite," said Sifu as he brushed his beard to the side, "we keep all that we learned. That is why I drank it. To absorb the knowledge, so it won't block you from learning more. Drink the tea, remember what you learned, but just make a little room for more."

"Ah, Sifu, I see," affirmed Ichi, as he nodded his head in understanding.

"Sifu, I need more knowledge. Can I have some more tea?" asked Lalo, as he held up his cup for another filling.

"Our mind needs to be open to new ideas. Is that right, Sifu?" asked Kekoa.

"Right. Sometimes new ways of doing things can be a benefit to us but we must be open to listening," remarked Sifu.

"Sifu, next time I am bringing two cups," exclaimed Shinji as he lifted up his cup, "I have a lot of room up there to fill."

"Yes, two cups," added Kekoa as she grabbed her cup and drank it down all at once, like Sifu. Without hesitation, Ichi did the same.

Sifu added, "Two cups! Haha! I like that!" as he brushed his beard to the side, "I can't wait for dessert!"

Exploring Mountain Temple

Located at the lower half of Fu Sheng Mountain, Mountain Temple looked as though it was as old as time itself. Built over 2,000 years ago, the walls of the temple have become home to various shades of deep green, crawling ivy and some of the walkway stepping stones have been nearly swallowed by the rich, thick, green moss.

Although you can hear the creaks and cracks of the centuries-old wooden floors, Mountain Temple has been considered to be one of the most skillfully designed structures ever built.

Many, many generations ago, when Mountain Temple was first constructed, the greatest and most skilled builders and craftsmen gave of themselves to create a structure that would stand the test of time.

The builders first put their effort into creating a

strong and powerful fortress.

Although established during a time of peace, the temple would later serve as a protective fortress. It would be a place where each of the nearby villages could take refuge and defend themselves against an oncoming enemy.

Once the walls and outside structures were completed, they turned their attention into creating the inside of the temple to be a learning center. The goal was for the monks to educate the people in a variety of subjects including art, culture, and martial arts training.

Understanding that the temple would in time, educate many of the children from the nearby villages, they designed it to be an extremely comfortable and welcoming environment.

Even more impressive, since several of the monks were inventors, they equipped the temple with the latest gadgets and inventions! Every year, to keep up-to-date with the world's latest technological breakthroughs, many of the monks traveled abroad to bring back the newest innovations.

For nearly two thousand years, it has been the tradition for the nearby villages to provide an opportunity for at least one child from each primary village to be educated and trained at Mountain Temple every year. In addition to their formal education, they would also learn the ways of the warrior and how to embrace their own heritage.

For these and many other reasons, the surrounding villages look toward Mountain Temple as an important part of their community and an essential part of their future.

For generation after generation, they have entrusted the monks to guide their young people and instill in them the values and necessary tools they will need in life. But most importantly, the children will learn about working together as a team and how they can benefit from each other.

Today, Mountain Temple is filled with over 20 monks, with some females as well as males.

The children will be assigned one monk as their primary teacher for a period of three to four years. The monk chosen for this particular group is Master Kong, who prefers to just be called "Sifu", which means teacher.

A great deal of preparation is done to ensure the children will be comfortable in their stay.

Unknown to the children, Sifu traveled to each village several months before their departure to Mountain Temple. He met with each student's parents so that he could learn about their likes and dislikes, their habits and favorite foods because, in a sense, he will fill the role of both their father and mother for many years.

The parents were also required to make several trips to Mountain Temple to not only familiarize themselves with the living conditions at the Temple, but to place several of the children's personal items in their rooms so that when they arrive, there would be a sense of familiarity.

Book One: The Adventures of Ichi and His Friends

The Chosen Few

Every year, the monks from Mountain Temple would meet with the elders of each village as well as the parents who feel their kids would benefit most from learning at the temple.

Traveling to Mountain Temple is a decision that both the child and parent must make together. No one is forced to leave their home. It is a mutual decision.

Throughout their young lives, the children will learn about Mountain Temple and the many opportunities it provides. However, no student is allowed to apply until they are at least eight years old. Most children going to the temple are usually 9 to 12 years of age.

Usually, one child from each village is selected.

These few children will leave their homes and travel a specific pathway to reach the temple. It will take them approximately five days to complete their journey.

Although the temple will be their home for several years, they are permitted to return to their village on special occasions, cultural celebrations and even when they get a little homesick. Parents and grandparents are encouraged to visit their children regularly.

Villages in the Nation of Siulum

Ichi and his friends lived in a more rustic and simple time period. The forms of transportation were primarily by horseback, horse-drawn carts, canoes, kayaks and sailboats. Water was brought to the village from man-made wells and the streets were paved with dirt and - in certain locations - cobblestone.

The standard of living has been modest for most of the villagers. They resided in either huts, wooden structures, tree houses or places made of stone.

Siulum

Although there were many small villages stretched across the Nation of Siulum, there were four much larger, primary villages.

Tomi Village – Ichi's home town, which stretches from the edge of the river and deep into the forest.

Kawa Village - Shinji's home town, which is on the edge of the forest but mostly against the river.

Waimea Village - This is Kekoa's home, which is a peninsula surrounded by two oceans.

Meiyo Village/Kingdom - This village is the furthest from Mountain Temple. Although it is in the forest, it is closer to the mountains. This largest of all the villages, in fact, it is twice as big as Tomi, Kawa and Waimea village combined. It is run by both a king and queen and is more commonly referred to as a Kingdom.

Each village is close to a day's ride from each other.

Preparing for the Long Journey

Sifu had coordinated specific dates and time periods for each child's departure. This ensured that the kids arrived at Mountain Temple at the same time.

Although the children believed that the pathway to Mountain Temple was simply the route they must take to reach their destination, it was actually the first step in their journey.

Each started their hike alone, but eventually met up along the way in order to build a friendship. Prior to their arrival at Mountain Temple, all four kids would be united.

Monks secretly disguised as villagers were placed along the way to provide assistance, if needed, but to also create unique opportunities for them as a learning experience.

In order to watch over the two youngest of the

travelers, Lalo and Shinji, Sifu arranged for "special en-counters" along the way so that their time alone would be very minimal.

Sifu provided each child with a special map that had specific stopping points along the way, which were usually small villages. The people from each of these hamlets worked with the monks of the Temple and were prepared to greet the little travelers.

At Mountain Temple, the children would not only be educated by the finest teachers, but they would travel together on a number of excursions and assigned specific tasks to help those in need.

They would learn to work with each other and in time, realize that together that can do almost anything. They would draw upon their strengths to help each other overcome their weaknesses. In turn, they would give Sifu something he did not know he truly needed: The family that he never had.

This is the story of the "Adventures of Ichi and his Friends".

A few weeks earlier...

Book One: The Adventures of Ichi and His Friends

Kekoa

Kekoa was born in one of the most exciting regions in the Nation of Siulum, the Village of Waimea. A peninsula, Waimea was surrounded by two very beautiful and extremely different beaches. On one side, the waves were gentle and calm and filled with the most beautiful coral reefs one could ever imagine. On the other side, it was like a roaring lion with waves so high that it was the ideal place for "hanging ten" on Kekoa's surfboard.

The people of Waimea were famous for hosting

the most enjoyable feasts and barbecues, as well as producing some of the greatest fighting warriors ever known.

Although Kekoa was the only girl in the group headed toward Mountain Temple, she was the most active of them all. A surfer since she could walk, she was considered one of the fastest and most powerful swimmers in the entire village.

She was quick, mobile and - of all the children - she was the most skilled in the martial arts. Her weapon of choice was the knuckle duster, which was a hand grip style weapon lined with shark-teeth!

Throughout her young life, Kekoa had excelled at everything she had tried. Although strong and tough, she did have a softer side. She was quite understanding and at times was very nurturing.

Kekoa was very traditional and enjoyed everything about her culture. From the music to the dancing, it was part of her soul. Like her mother, and her mother before her, she was an avid, traditional dancer sharing the stories of her ancestors in her dance movements.

Only 10 years old, her wisdom had become her strength. Kekoa was a great listener and had a knack for planning strategies rather than blindly rushing into a situation.

She was very close to her Grandma Oda and would often stay with her for days at a time.

Kekoa enjoyed wearing face paint and traditional jewelry.

Grandma Oda

It was late into the evening as the crickets began their nightly melody by rubbing their feet together. Kekoa and her grandmother were working by candlelight to put the finishing touches on the Ancestry Shells for the upcoming Ohana Festival.

A time-honored tradition, the Ohana Festival has been part of her village for longer than her grandmother could remember.

Every year, for two whole weeks, the entire village gathered together to remember family and those that have come before them. The Ohana Festival was also a very special time for Grandma Oda. Why? Because it was at that very festival where she met her future husband, Kaihewalu Oda.

"Grandma Oda, I really enjoy spending time together making these lovely shell strings with you," said Kekoa looking through a bag of shells she gathered earlier in the day.

"Preparing for the festival is just as important as the event itself," said Grandma Oda, as she covered the table with a cloth.

"Why's that?" expressed Kekoa, as she pulled out a few good shells from her bag.

"Because with each seashell we write the name of one of our ancestors," responded Grandma Oda, as she turned over one of the shells onto its smoother side. "Look here, this one has my mother's name and this one over here has her mother's name. By writing down their names on each shell, we keep our history alive. Through these simple sea shells, we can trace our family tree for

43

hundreds of years," remarked Grandma Oda, as she joined Kekoa looking for some nice shells.

"Really?" responded Kekoa with a great big smile as she examined both sides of the shell. "What was your mom's name?"

"It was Tichia Nava," replied Grandma Oda. "Oh, she was such a fun and very special mother. I loved her so much," as she held the shell with great affection and brought it closer to her heart.

"Then, if she's your mom, that would make her my great-grandma right," said Kekoa with great anticipation.

"That's right," replied Grandma Oda, "Now child, get me some of those long strings from the cabinet."

"This one, grandma?" said Kekoa as she pointed to the middle shelf.

"Yes, those strong ones," confirmed Grandma Oda. "We take this long string and then we carefully tie each shell to it. It must be very secure, so we add a little tree glue to make sure they won't fall off. We have a long family history, so it may take about four strands this year."

Each strand was attached to a long, five-foot stick which made it easier to carry and enabled it to be hung on a special place in the town square. When all the strings of shells were hung next to each other, they resembled a huge white waterfall.

Everyone throughout the village would be participating in this same tradition, each representing their own family line.

"Boy, this is so exciting! I have never actually known the full meaning of the Ancestry Shells!" exclaimed Kekoa as she sanded down the edge of one of the rougher shells.

"When the wind blows, you can hear the shells chiming all across the village. Many say that for each of those moments, the memories of those before us can be felt a little deeper in their hearts."

"Now look here dear," Grandma Oda pointed to the last shell that she was about to hang on the family string. "This final shell right here, this represents you."

Grandma Oda then wrote down Kekoa's name on it!

"Me?!" responded Kekoa as her eyes lit up with pride.

Grandma Oda took the shell with special care, gave it a few drops of glue and wrapped it securely on the string since this was now the last shell in the family line.

"Today, Kekoa, you will take your place in history, as I did when I was your age," Grandma Oda explained. "Tomorrow, we'll bring our ancestry strands together with the entire village. Oh, it will be a sight to see! There will be music and dancing and storytelling. It will be wonderful!"

"I love the dancing! It's so much fun," expressed Kekoa.

"Oh, it's very exciting. We all gather into circles, one bigger than the next, and we all dance together. You know your grandma used to be pretty good herself," as Grandma Oda picked up a broom and began dancing in a circle. "La, la, lala."

"Every dance has a special meaning. The waving of the hands represents the journey across the ocean. Each step represents the path of the warrior. In fact, your great, great grandfather fought many battles," Grandma Oda added proudly.

"His stories are still told today in our dances."

"His name was Makuota, but they all called him 'Maku the Mighty'," said Grandma Oda as she placed her fist against her heart and stood up a little straighter. "I think of all your ancestors, you take after him the most."

"Really? Tell me more about him, grandma," pleaded Kekoa, as she leaned forward in her chair.

"My Grandpa Maku was a very, very skilled warrior. He was one of the greatest leaders of our tribe. He was brave and very handsome and he had such great accuracy with a bow. In fact, he was so good he was able to hit the pineapple right in the center! Every time!" motioned Grandma Oda.

"That's just like me!" Kekoa exclaimed, with her tongue out and hands pulled back as if she were shooting an arrow. "Every time I use my bow and arrow, I always hit the pineapple right in the center!"

"There were many wars back then and your great, great grandpa Maku helped keep this village safe," said Grandma Oda proudly, as a smile appeared on her face. "He was the mighty of the mighty, just like you," as Grandma Oda then gently put her index finger on Kekoa's forehead.

Kekoa stood a little straighter and lifted her shoulders high, to show respect as she copied the salute her grandma made earlier.

"Child, it is now your turn to be the one to represent our village," Grandma Oda said in an encouraging tone. "In time, it will fall to you to teach our people the ways of the warrior and keep our culture and traditions alive."

"When you take your journey to Mountain Temple in a short while, you will experience some wonderful and amazing things," Grandma Oda added.

With a curious look on her face, Kekoa asked, "Grandma, you took the journey to Mountain Temple, too. When you were my age, right?"

"Yes, honey," Grandma Oda confirmed. "I was the same age as you are today. My mother wanted me to wait for another year. But I was too excited!"

"You know, your grandma was quite a handful then!" she exclaimed while laughing as she grabbed the arm of the rocking chair and sat down. "It was quite an adventure!"

"How long were you there grandma?"

"I studied with Sifu Fong for over five years," nodded Grandma Oda as she looked into the sky as if it was filled with memories. "Child, it was the best time of my life."

"You know, you can stay at Mountain Temple as long as you like. I stayed there a little longer than most until I felt confident that I learned everything I needed to know," Grandma Oda continued. "Oh, it was hard at first though! A lot of studying. A lot of practicing, traveling and really roughing it out at times.

"Back then, the war was still going on and I was

even caught up in a few battles. Sometimes I didn't think I would make it! But my classmates, my family, were there for me," confessed Grandma Oda as she got up, grabbed her broom and swung it in the air like a twenty-year-old.

"Way to go, grandma!" said Kekoa, as they laughed together.

"Child, you are going to learn so much," said Grandma Oda. "Like me, your classmates are going to be your family as well."

"But I will miss our times together," confessed Kekoa, with a bit of sadness in her expression.

"Well, that's the beauty of Mountain Temple," explained Grandma Oda. "You can come home on special occasions and I can come and visit any time I desire. It's not a monastery! It is a place of learning and growing."

"Really, grandma?" expressed Kekoa with relief.

"Oh yes dear," Grandma Oda agreed as she held out the long string of Ancestry Shells. "Now honey, let's double-check all the names and make sure the shells are nice and secure. Then we'll hang them up right here, so they will be ready for tomorrow."

Sifu's Map

It was an early, brisk morning on the day Kekoa was to begin her journey to Mountain Temple. Sifu had created a series of special maps for the young travelers. Every one of them was laced with specific stopping points along the way.

All of the children started their adventure on foot, each carrying a large backpack containing some of their individual, personal items. Although nearly everything would be provided for them at the Temple, they were asked to pack some clothes for both winter and summer.

"Now child, I know Sifu made all you kids brand new maps," said Grandma Oda as she walked to the cabinet, grabbed her old map off one of the shelves and blew on it as the dust flied everywhere.

"But look here! This is the map I used when I traveled to Mountain Temple," revealed Grandma Oda. "I kept it just in case it would be used by another member of our family. I jotted down some notes here on the edges of my map that may come in handy during your trip."

The sea weather had taken its toll on grandma's map. The corners were yellowed and the folds revealed some small cracks.

"Oooh! This very exciting," exclaimed Kekoa as she moved closer to her Grandma Oda and they both looked at her notes together.

"Yes indeedy! Oh my, this map brings back so many memories," remarked Grandma Oda as she graced her hand across the map, ironing out the creases and unfolding the corners. "In case you change your mind, I can take your place," she remarked as they both laughed.

"See this here. There are some nice places to go for some water and some edible plants can be found over here," Grandma Oda pointedly said, as she guided her finger across the map.

"Of course, it's been many years and those plants may be gone by now, but you never know!"

"Grandma, what are these notes over here? It has what looks like, a heart on it!"

"Let me see that honey," Grandma Oda said as she leaned closer to the map to get a better look. "Oh my! Oh my, my, my!" as she smiled. "This, my dear child..." she managed to get out, her cheeks becoming as red as a rose, "...this was from a small village that I visited a long, long time ago. It was called the Village of Keena. I had spent a little time there on my journey to Mountain Temple and it was there that I met this young boy."

"His name was Manu, Grandma Oda continued. "Oh, he was so nice and very cute! We only spent just a day or so together but you never forget your first kiss."

"Grandma!?!" exclaimed Kekoa, with a shocked smile on her face, as Grandma Oda's cheeks continued to blush while recalling her memory. "He's probably gone by now but it would have been nice just to know how he's doing," Grandma Oda said wistfully, before looking more closely at Sifu's map.

"Now according to this map, eventually you will visit Shang Na village. There are some great eating places there. I was there about six months ago and I can still taste that wonderful sauce dip I put on my fish! Yummy!"

Preparing for Her Journey

You could hear the roar of the ocean in the distance as Kekoa, Grandma Oda and Kekoa's father and mother all enjoyed a final breakfast together for at least some time. "Kekoa," said Waiola, her mother, "it's almost time for you to begin your journey. Have you packed everything you need, honey?"

"Yes mom, I'm so packed I could barely carry my backpack," said Kekoa, as she struggled slightly strapping on her pack. "Boy, this is a little heavy!"

"Be sure you packed some extra underwear," said Grandma Oda.

"I put in five extra just in case," Kekoa said laughing. "I also packed my swimsuit! I know there's a nice lake not far from the temple so I might do a little swimming there."

"I won't take my board because I don't think they have many waves up there."

Waiola struggled with feelings of both joy for Kekoa's trip, but also concern.

"Now honey, be sure to be safe. Stay on the path that Sifu made for you and try to get plenty of rest along the way," said Waiola. "This is not a race to Mountain Temple you know. You take your time and you will meet up with your soon-to-be classmates along the way and you will all travel together."

"Your journey is part of the adventure my dear," her father, Kimo, pointed out. "Be sure to write to us and let us know how you are doing and don't be afraid to ask for help."

"I won't! Daddy, mom, grandma. I will miss you all so much," confessed Kekoa with a bit of sadness mixed with excitement, as all three of them hugged together.

"Oh my granddaughter, we will see you in just a few weeks when you are all settled in at the open-house at Mountain Temple. We'll be staying overnight so save one of the nicer rooms for me," said Grandma Oda as she gave Kekoa another big hug and tons of kisses.

Kimo took a few moments to double-check her backpack, to make sure that everything was nice and secure. Then he said, "Your cousin Lelani wanted us to give you this for your journey. It may come in handy," as he clipped a leather water sack to her waist.

The family walked with Kekoa out the door and continued with her as she started her walk on the trail.

"Well, here I go! Wish me luck," said Kekoa, with a half-smile. "Love ya and see you in a few weeks!"

Kekoa's Adventure Begins

Kekoa continued to wave back at her parents and Grandma Oda as she walked along the dirt pathway leading her toward Mountain Temple.

Finding a few places to rest along the way, Kekoa enjoyed admiring the countryside of Siulum. About six hours into her trip, Kekoa found a large boulder to sit upon as she slipped off her right shoe. She turned it upside down and banged it against a rock a few times until a small pebble eventually lodged free and fell to the ground.

"Aah! Now, that feels so much better," muttered Kekoa to herself, smiling like she just won a contest! "For the last 10 minutes, I thought I felt something bothering my foot! Now, I know."

Kekoa put her shoe back on and climbed to the top of the boulder. With her hands placed on her hips, she took a deep breath and began to look around.

"Wow, will you look at this! It's so beautiful here," Kekoa said out loud with admiration, as she turned in a circle to take in the scenery. "I've been out here many times before but I never took the time to notice these magnificent trees and those awesome mountains! Having to walk gives me time to admire nature up close! It's just wonderful!"

As Kekoa sat down to admire the view, she unfastened the leather pouch that had been filled with cold water for her to enjoy. Her cousin Lelani had hand-made two very special pouches; one for herself and one for Kekoa. It would not only keep the water cool, but it was also easy to carry.

She held the pouch up high and gulped down some refreshing water that quenched her thirst. "Thank you cousin Lelani," thought Kekoa.

As she sat there, Kekoa pulled out her map and noticed that Shang Na Village was still a couple of days away. It would be dark in a few hours so she would need to find a place to sleep and rest her weary body for the night. Sifu had designated a special place on the map where Kekoa was able to camp.

Kekoa continued on her path until dusk was nearly upon her.

About 100 feet ahead, she noticed a small, but quaint little camping area. It was an ideal spot for settling in for the night. The camping area was equipped with a blanket-covered hammock, a small circle of rocks for a campfire and a series of hooks. The hooks were suspended by a rope, in between two trees, so that she was able to hang her backpack and other items she may have been carrying.

"Well, if I didn't know better, I would think that they prepared this little ol' spot just for me," Kekoa said, smiling.

Settling comfortably into her hammock, she saw

thousands upon thousands of stars fill the night sky. One after another, the shooting stars continued to race across the heavens and just like counting sheep, the streaking stars helped Kekoa fall fast asleep.

The rays from the morning sun became Kekoa's alarm clock.

"Wow!" she exclaimed. "That was a great night's sleep. This was my first time in a hammock and it was pretty nice! I will have to get me one of these!"

After making herself a little breakfast, she once again pulled out her map and studied her pathway.

"Hmm, it looks like I'll be traveling a little further today," she said. "It says I'm supposed to go through this area," Kekoa then moved her finger across the map, talking out loud as she did so.

"Then, I take this path to the right, then up this area here, then across this small river and then into this small little town to spend two nights with this elderly couple."

Kekoa then refolded the map and put it back into her pack.

Throughout the day, she encountered many of the inhabitants along the way. Unknown to her, Sifu had arranged specific villagers to watch over her so that she would have company during several parts of her journey, thus providing an opportunity to learn about the lives of the village people.

"Oh look, that must be the small village where I'm supposed to stay," said Kekoa. "Keena Village! Hmmm, why does that name sound familiar?"

An elderly man was standing at the edge of what

seemed like a very quaint little town. The man was tall, with gray hair and he was waving his hat to get Kekoa's attention!

"Hey, young lady," the man said. "You look like a weary traveler so I'm guessing you must be young Kekoa?"

"Hi! Yes I am," she said. "You must be the people I'm supposed to be staying with tonight."

"You are correct," the man replied.

This had to be one of the earliest towns ever built. The buildings seemed like they were hundreds of years old. Weathered by time, they even boasted some scars of the previous wars. Just then, an elderly woman came out from her home and waved to Kekoa.

"Well, well," the elderly woman said. "We are always thrilled to help out Sifu and any of his candidates that are taking the journey to Mountain Temple. My name is Noemi and this old relic is my loving husband, Manu."

"We got some nice and hot food ready for you. So come on in, put your stuff down and have some grub, little lady," said Noemi.

Kekoa bowed to the couple and put her backpack in the corner of the room. She then took a seat at the supper table and grabbed a spoon to taste the soup.

"Mmm, mmm! This is delicious Auntie Noemi. It tastes just like mom's food!" exclaimed Kekoa, with a smile on her face and some soup still on her lips.

"That's because Sifu had brought us your mom's recipe!" confessed Noemi.

"Whoa! How cool is that!" added Kekoa, "I like this Sifu already. He's got style."

Manu and Noemi had been working with the monks of Mountain Temple for over a hundred years.

After taking a few sips of soup, Manu paused for a moment and said, "I recall my father was very involved with the monks, ever since I was little. Oh, over the years I have seen many young travelers stopping here."

"That's amazing Uncle Manu," remarked Kekoa, as she sipped up the last bit of her soup.

After they finished their evening meal, Kekoa and the elderly couple went into the living room where they sat in front of a roaring fire as they shared the history of Keena Village and how the fighting of the war made it all the way to their doorstep.

"Oh yes, me and mama have been around a very long time, so we've got a lot of stories to tell! We've seen it all and we were part of it all as well," added Manu.

"My husband's family has been serving Mountain Temple for longer than me. He can tell you so much more than I can. Hey Manu, do you remember that young girl that really rocked your world?" Noemi chuckled, while leaning back in her rocking chair.

"Oh, yes!" recalled Manu as a smile came across his face and he began to comb his hair. "I still remember her! She was a lovely girl! Around your age, Kekoa! In fact, I think she came from Waimea Village."

"Hey, yes, that's where I'm from," exclaimed Kekoa, as her hair on the back of her neck began to stand up with a tinge of excitement.

"It was a very, very long time ago. Her name was Kiwani, yes, Kiwani Oda was her name," recalled Manu. She was my first kiss! Wow! What a wonderful girl she was!" he said, with a boyish, shy look on his face.

"Wait a minute! Wait just a minute," wondered Kekoa, as she pulled out her map and put it in front of the candle to see more clearly. "Is this the Village of Keena?"

"Yep, it sure is," said Noemi.

"Kiwani Oda is my Grandma Oda! It's you! You are Manu! You were her first kiss! Wow, what a small world," smiled Kekoa.

"Kiwani is your grandmother!?" Manu exclaimed with both excitement and shock.

"Oh this is too funny," confessed Kekoa. "Grandma just talked about you the other day. She was wondering how you were doing and truly missed her time together with you."

After two more strokes with his comb, Manu put it in his back pocket and said, "Now that I look at your face more closely, I can see your grandma's eyes in you. You tell your grandma hello for me and thank her for her kindness."

"I will. She will be so excited," concluded Kekoa. Kekoa would spend a second day with Manu and Noemi as they took her through the forest, pointed out where many of the battles were fought and even where Manu and Grandma Oda had their first kiss.

"It was an honor to stay with you," she said, while bowing to both of them.

"Goodbye, Auntie Noemi. Goodbye Uncle Manu. Thanks to you both," Kekoa said, as she resumed her quest.

With a final hug, Manu leaned and whispered in

Kekoa's ear, "Don't forget to tell Kiwani hello for me."

"I won't forget," Kekoa whispered back in response.

Reaching Shang Na Village

About a half-day after her departure from Keena Village, Kekoa found a nice place to rest. She pulled out her water pouch and quenched her thirst once again, having found a fallen tree to sit on.

She couldn't help but notice the peacefulness of her surroundings. She took out her map again and examined the route that was designed for her trek. After about five minutes, she folded it up again, put it in her back pocket and restarted her expedition.

"Although I've been walking for a long time," Kekoa admitted to herself, "it's actually very refreshing." She continued on her sojourn until the evening, when the trail led her to a small town along the river called Shang Na Village. Although it seemed like a more rustic place, you could smell the sweet aroma of the many delicacies cooking throughout the marketplace.

As she got further into the village, she noticed that it was filled with activity around the marketplace as the townspeople were making deals and conversing. But it was the sound of Kekoa's hungry stomach that seemed the loudest of them all.

"Fresh fish, get your fresh fish here!" screamed out the deli-man in a small shop just across the street.

"Oh, I love fresh fish! Yummy," she exclaimed as she licked her lips in anticipation.

As Kekoa walked toward the deli-shop, an old lady

in a horse-drawn carriage was coming in her direction. "Please go ahead auntie," she said as she waited patiently until the old lady passed her. "Thank you dearie," said the woman, while she waved to Kekoa.

"Hi, Missy," remarked the deli-man as he finished squeezing some lemon on a meal he was serving. "My fish are so fresh they are practically jumping from the river right into my shop," said the deli-man, without a hint of modesty. "Would you like to enjoy one today? I'll cook 'em up right here!"

"Would I?!" Kekoa responded with enthusiasm. "My stomach says make it fast and delicious!"

"Sszzzzz!" was the sound of the fish hitting the grill. Slicing like a true artist, the deli-man looked to Kekoa and said, "Young lady, too bad you weren't here last night. Wow! We had a big celebration! There was singing and dancing. It was a lot of fun!"

"Oh too bad, that does sounds like fun!" she said excitedly.

The deli-man grabbed a plate, placed the fish in the center, squeezed a few slices of lemon and topped it off with a little garnish to give it some beauty and provided a cup of his secret sauce.

"There you go, Missy!" he said loudly.

"Hmm, that smells great! I hope it tastes as wonderful as it smells," remarked Kekoa, with fork and knife in each hand. In less than five minutes, she finished her entire meal, garnish and all!"

"Wow, that was the fastest I've seen anyone eat! You must have been starved," remarked the deli-man.

"Well, you did say it would be delicious and so it

was!" exclaimed Kekoa, as she wiped her mouth with a napkin. "It was very fresh and that sauce, it was to die for, just like grandma said."

Kekoa paid the deli-man, pulled back on her chair and strapped her pack back on. She then headed out the door in the direction of the other shops.

"It's getting late so I'd better do some quick shopping," she said to herself.

Throughout the next hour, Kekoa enjoyed her time in the marketplace, where she made bargains and looked for unique items to buy - until she came across a snack store!

"Excuse me sir, but do you have any peanuts available?" Kekoa asked the storekeeper hopefully.

"Do I have peanuts?" he asked in a rhetorical manner.

He escorted her to the center of the store and revealed ten barrels filled to the top with peanuts.

"Let me see....we have extra-large peanuts, round peanuts, salty peanuts, green peanuts, spicy peanuts...." exclaimed the storekeeper, as he went through every variety of peanut he had in stock.

"Okay! Okay! I think I get the idea," Kekoa exclaimed while laughing.

"But wait! We also have chocolate-covered peanuts, ginger peanuts and...", continued the storekeeper, until he was finally interrupted by Kekoa.

"I'll just take the large peanuts?" added Kekoa.

"Not very adventurous are you?" said the storekeeper as he rubbed his chin. "So, then, how many bags do you want? Eight? Ten?" asked the storekeeper, now hoping to get a big sale.

"Just one bag of large peanuts please," replied Kekoa, politely but firmly. She took out her change purse to pay the man, then stuffed the bag into her backpack.

"This isn't for me, it's for a friend or someone I hope will be a friend," Kekoa said. "I was told he loves this stuff and a bag of peanuts might be a nice 'hello' gift."

"Two bags would be a 'hello gift' and three bags would be a 'how do you do' gift," challenged the store-keeper as he was ready to fill another bag for Kekoa.

"I think this will be fine, thank you," as she left the marketplace and headed toward her sleeping quarters for the night, the Mulan Inn.

Tragedy on the Old Trail

Early the next morning, Kekoa continued her journey to Mountain Temple. Reaching the far end of Shang Na Village, she came upon a divided road.

According to her map, she was to take the pathway on the left. The one leading into the forest!

About five miles into her excursion, she noticed an old woman in a cart about 100 yards ahead. In fact, the cart was so old, you could hear the creaks and cracks a mile away.

"Hey, I remember seeing that cart back at the village!" thought Kekoa, "She isn't that far away, so I should be able to catch up to her soon."

As she drew nearer to the cart, the creaks were getting louder and then, all of a sudden, one of the wheels started wobbling back and forth!

"Oh no!" exclaimed Kekoa. She dropped her backpack and began a sprint toward the old woman.

"Aiyaah!" cried out the old woman as the cart started to buckle and one of the four wheels came completely off.

"I've got to get there quickly," thought Kekoa as the old woman's horse panicked and started knocking the woman from side to side.

The old woman dropped the reins and just as she was about to fall over, Kekoa reached out her arms to catch her. "I got you!" shouted Kekoa.

But just when Kekoa had thought she had rescued the old woman, the horse buckled again and knocked the cart in their direction. Now they both needed to be rescued!

All of a sudden, two hands came from out of nowhere and grabbed the cart and pulled it back safely to the ground. "Whoa horsey," said a voice from the other side of the cart, as the horse began to settle down.

"You two ladies doing okay?" yelled out a young man's voice."

"That was too close," fretted Kekoa.

"You said it," remarked the young man with a smile on his face. "You must be Kekoa," he added, "Haha! Yes! You must be Ichi," said Kekoa with delight. "I knew we were supposed to meet up, but I didn't think it was going to be like this."

"Well, thank you again, young lady! And thank you, as well, young gentleman," said the old lady. "I don't know what would have happened if you two hadn't come along like you did."

Ichi

Ichi is the eldest of the children venturing to Mountain Temple. He was born in the Village of Tomi, which is a very traditional community. Tomi's boundaries lie from the edge of the river into a vast forest filled with towering and beautiful pine trees.

The people of the village are very close and very family-oriented. Each and every month, the people gathered together, made campfires and shared stories of long ago. Family is the most important thing to them, as it is with Ichi.

Ichi is 11 years old. Kekoa is 10. Lalo and Shinji are 9. Ichi could have joined Mountain Temple years earlier. However, he knew that his young cousin, Shinji, had also planned to take the journey when he was old enough. So Ichi decided to wait for him so that they could attend Mountain Temple together.

Shinji lived in a nearby village called Kawa. He and his cousin were very close. They were more like brothers than cousins. Besides, his mother always reminded him, "Be sure to look out for your little cousin, Shinji."

Although very young, Ichi was considered one of the most highly skilled experts in swordsmanship. After all, his father was his teacher! So, he began learning the arts at a very young age.

In fact, he was so accurate with the sword, the kids often threw an apple to him just so he would cut it in half!

Ichi was also well versed in the classical arts. A painter, a poet, a musician and a singer, Ichi was a man of many talents.

Although a little more on the serious side at times, he was also very funny and playful. He loved a good story and like Sifu, he enjoyed his food.

Ichi's biggest weakness was peanuts, which he absolutely loved. So much so, that everyone in Mountain Temple knew that when they really wanted him to go along with something, they could easily bribe him with a bag of peanuts!

Ichi, the Swordsman

"Swordsmanship is a very traditional and beautiful art form to study. As your arm is part of your body, the sword must be an extension of you as well," explained Toshi, Ichi's father and teacher. "The sword should always be treated with great respect."

Toshi looked at the bowl full of apples on the table in front of him. He picked one up, looked at it carefully, then tossed it up high into the air.

Like a bolt of lightning - yet as smooth as silk - he drew his sword. Swoosh! Swoosh again and Again! He sliced it into four perfect pieces. He picked up the four pieces and threw them to some nearby squirrels who seemed to have been patiently waiting for a handout.

With his mouth opened wide in amazement, Ichi remarked, "Wow! That's awesome, father!"

"Now, it's your turn," challenged Toshi, as he grabbed another apple from the bowl. While he did so, another two squirrels decided to join in on the treats.

"You've cut an apple into two equal parts, many times," encouraged his father. "Now, it's time you put your skill to the test by cutting the apple into four equal pieces. I know you can do it!"

"Ready son?" questioned Toshi, as he held the apple in his hand and prepared to throw it into the air.

"Ready," remarked Ichi, as he tried to keep his breathing smooth and steady.

Toshi brought his hand low and then tossed the apple up into the air!

Ichi placed his hand on the sword, as he waited for the apple to begin its descent.

Although it seemed like 10 minutes, the apple finally started to come down toward down Ichi in mere seconds.

As he was anxiously waiting, a few drops of perspiration started to bead on Ichi's forehead.

Like he was one with the blade, Ichi then took a firm grip on the handle and swiftly pulled out the sword.

As he leaned slightly forward he sliced in an upward angle as he cut the apple in two!

The squirrels also looked up to the sky with their mouths wide open as if they exclaimed "Ooooh!" Then, just before the apple had a chance to divide, the sword continued in a slight loop as Ichi slashed upward again and sliced the apple into four equal pieces.

The little squirrels grabbed a piece each for themselves and scurried back into the forest to eat their meal. Ichi placed the sword ever-so-carefully back into its holder.

He then took a moment as he breathed out slowly, then jumped up and exclaimed, "I did it! I did it!" With barely enough air in his lungs he shouted, "I cut the apple into fours!"

"Well done my son! Well done!" exclaimed his father, who could barely control his own excitement.

"Cutting the apple into fours is an example of balancing your mind and body," explained Toshi. "The softness is the smoothness with which you pulled out the sword. The hardness is the sword striking the apple and cutting it into pieces. One must use that balance to their advantage."

"Like the yin and the yang symbol. One is black

the other is white. One is soft, the opposite is hard," Ichi said, as realization dawned on him.

"Right you are son," said Toshi. "In time, you will be able to pull out the blade more smoothly and be even more fluid! This will help your accuracy a great deal."

"I see," Ichi said, nodding as he did so.

"To improve your smoothness, you need to apply yourself to practicing painting, so that your arms flow more freely. You need to learn how to play a musical instrument, so your fingers become more light and quick! You also need to learn how to act in plays and learn how to dance to make the body more fluid," encouraged Toshi.

"I am very proud of your decision to delay your journey to Mountain Temple, in order to wait for your little cousin Shinji. You know, he really looks up to you! Helping him on this journey will be great for both of you," Toshi added.

"His father and I, like you and your cousin, are not only brothers, but we are the best of friends! Your Uncle Fumio and I did everything together and even though we don't see each other as often as I would like, I still feel close to him," concluded Toshi.

The Preparation Begins

Ichi's village, Tomi, was in the opposite direction of Kekoa's home town of Waimea. So Sifu had to time his departure just right, in order to ensure that Ichi and Kekoa were the first to meet up on the trail, which was just outside of Shang Na Village.

Baloop! Fizzz! Szzz! were the sounds that woke

Ichi's mother Rumiko early that morning.

"Huh? What's that noise?" asked Rumiko, as she got out of bed and walked into the kitchen.

There she spotted Ichi, huddled over a hot stove, as he was preparing a very, very early breakfast snack.

"Hello, my son! What are you doing up so early? It's not even breakfast time! You should go back to bed! You need to rest up, you have a long trip ahead of you," said Rumiko, as she gave out a big yawn.

"I just wanted to be extra prepared and make sure I didn't forget anything. So, I packed my bags early and decided to grab a snack," remarked Ichi. "I'll see Cousin Shinji later in the week - and you know how he forgets! So I'm packing a few extra things for him. Let's see. I got an extra toothbrush, just in case. Some licorice, for both of us. Last but not least, we cannot forget my favorite."

"Peanuts," said Rumiko and Ichi in unison.

"You got it! I got some roasted peanuts, salted peanuts, unsalted peanuts, and spicy peanuts!" exclaimed Ichi, as he pulled out another bag of peanuts from the cabinet.

"Think I packed enough peanuts? Just to be on the safe side, don't want to run out. Maybe just one bag more for Shinji."

"Well that's very nice of you thinking of your cousin, but it's so early Ichi," reminded Rumiko with her eyes barely open.

"Yeah, I know, but I'm so excited about the journey that I just can't sleep," exclaimed Ichi as he continued to pack his backpack.

"And mom, I packed some extra underwear just

in case," Ichi said, with a smile on his face.

Just then, Toshi calmly yelled out from the hallway, "Hey, who's making all the noise out there!?

It's so early in the morning that the rooster hasn't even crowed yet!" Toshi exclaimed, as he let out a big yawn.

"Hi dear," said Rumiko, as Toshi wiped his eyes and slid his feet down the hallway like a zombie. Toshi made an effort to give Rumiko a kiss on the cheek but failed because he was so sleepy.

"So, what's going on?" mumbled Toshi.

"Morning, dad! I couldn't sleep! I'm so excited! I finished packing, again, and I started to make a little breakfast snack," exclaimed Ichi.

"Oh, I see," Toshi said. He then paused for a moment, scratching his head with his eyes still mostly closed. "Okay," he said simply, as he headed back to the bedroom. He entered dreamland in midair, right before his body hit the bed.

"Well, I guess I will join you for a breakfast snack, as you call it," Rumiko said, as she pulled out one of the chairs and sat down at the table.

"Here you go! I made an extra egg, just in case," said Ichi, while motioning to Rumiko. He served a little scrambled egg on her plate. "Hmm, smell that! It tastes just as good as it smells!"

"Well, it smells delicious," Rumiko said, as she took a bite. "It's even more delicious than it smells," Rumiko continued, with a surprised look on her face. "Wow, it's really delicious. I have to admit something. I taught you everything I know, but you took it a step further. You seem to make every dish more delicious than I could imagine Chef Ichi! They are going to love your cooking at Mountain Temple!"

"Thank you, mom. It's my additional spices that make it special," explained Ichi with great pride. "Oh, that reminds me, I've got to bring some spices for our meals. Yes, some vanilla spices would be nice! Maybe some sweet chocolate would really blow their taste buds!"

Ichi then grabbed a bunch of spices, put them in a bag and loaded them into his backpack. "Well, I'll just take the lot of them! You never can tell which ones will go over well," he said.

"Oh dear, your bag is starting to look a little full, perhaps you should only take just one or two spices and let that be it. You don't want to rip your bag," stressed Rumiko, as she lifted up his bag and felt it's weight.

"It's a little heavy, but that's why I got this extra bag. I can just attach them to each other so it won't be too bulky," explained Ichi as he held out a smaller, additional bag.

"Honey, it's five in the morning and you won't be leaving for at least another six hours or so. Why don't you put your pack down and try to get some rest?"

"Well," sighed Ichi, with a long pause. "I guess you're right, I can only do so much, you know."

"Yes, son," said his mother, as she escorted Ichi back to his bed. "I know you are very excited and so are we! But you need to try and get some rest."

"I just don't think I can sleep, mom," warned Ichi. He began to lay down on his bed, as his mom tucked him in.

"Honey, just give it a shot" said Rumiko as her words were suddenly cut short by a series of loud snores.

Ichi had fallen fast asleep!

After a couple of hours, both his father and mother got out of bed and started eating together.

"Should we wake him?" Rumiko asked her husband.

"Nah, his excitement wore him out! Let him sleep for a couple more hours," he replied. "He won't get much sleep on the road to Mountain Temple."

"You know, he snores just like you," laughed Rumiko.

Several hours passed by and Ichi started to awaken. He rubbed his eyes and remarked out loud, "See, I told you I wasn't sleepy," as he stretched his arms out and yawned. "I didn't sleep a wink."

His mother and father began to laugh.

Ichi Takes His First Step

A few hours later, Rumiko and Toshi joined Ichi as they walked to the beginning of the trail to Mountain Temple. "Ichi, as you take your first step, you continue the legacy of our family and our people," expressed Toshi.

"This is a wonderful chapter in your life," added Rumiko. "You will have so much fun and you will learn some amazing things. Life will be hard sometimes, but be sure to lean on and trust in your companions. Some of them will be part of your life forever! Your great Aunt Ishii was a student of Mountain Temple and when she was on the council, one of her advisors was a fellow student from the temple."

"Really!" explained Ichi, with an inspired look on his face, "I didn't know that mother. How exciting!"

Ichi turned to his father and gave him a hug and then turned to his mother. She confessed to him, "I will miss you, my son." Then she added, "But don't forget to take care of your cousin Shinji."

"I won't forget, mom," replied Ichi. "I won't disappoint you."

"Okay, my boy! We will see you in a couple of weeks at the temple during your open house," said Toshi.

"When you do, don't forget to bring some more peanuts," Ichi reminded them.

"Be sure to send a letter to let us know how you are doing!" exclaimed Rumiko as she gave him a final hug.

"I won't forget! I will write to you and give you all the details," said Ichi as he started his walk on the trail with a final wave back to his parents.

As Ichi's figure began to fade in the distance, Rumiko leaned against her husband as he put his arm around her. She said in a soft tone, "I miss him already."

Ichi's Path to Mountain Temple

"According to Sifu's instructions, since Kekoa and I are the eldest, we will be spending a little camping time in the wilderness," Ichi said to himself, as he walked along the trail for the next five hours.

"Whew! Boy, this has been a long walk," remarked Ichi, as he stopped along the path to take a drink from his water pouch. "Aaah! That was good!" he exclaimed.

Ichi then looked at his map to determine where he was. "Hmm. I'm supposed to spend tonight under the stars, he said. 'It looks like the sun will set in about two hours and there's supposed to be a nice area up ahead to set up camp."

It wasn't long before Ichi found the camping area that was prepared for him, complete with hammock and blanket.

Ichi took off his backpack and tested the durability of the hammock. After he heard the sound of a flowing river nearby, he got up and took a stroll in it's direction.

He went about 100 feet and there, before him, was a beautiful, crystal blue lake that the river had formed. Climbing on top of a very large boulder that was halfway into the water, he could see that the lake was so clear he could actually see the bottom.

"Oh, this is too exciting to pass up!" Ichi said anxiously to himself, gazing at such an open invitation. Without hesitation, he took off his shoes, threw his shirt to the ground, took a few steps back and sprinted to the top of the boulder!

Although he knew the lake - being out here in the middle of the wilderness - was going to be freezing cold, he didn't care. When he reached the top, he did a cannonball jump and "SPLASH!" he landed right into the chilly, but refreshing, water.

The cold water was a welcome treat to his tired body. Ichi enjoyed his time splishing and splashing in the water for at least an hour.

"Well, that was fun! I guess it's time to dry off and

set up camp," he said to himself.

Spssss! The frying pan sizzled, as Ichi started to cook his first away-from-home meal. You could smell the sweet aroma of fresh, delicious and soon-to-be-eaten grub. Ichi's mom had packed some fresh food so that it would stay frozen for hours, just enough time so that it would be ready for him to enjoy.

"Mom thinks of everything!" Ichi rejoiced out loud.

A nearby squirrel came to pay him a visit as Ichi put together a few morsels for the little one to enjoy. "Hey, I think I know your cousins back home," he said to the squirrel.

As Ichi settled in for the night, he recalled all the beautiful colors of the forest he had seen along the way. He remembered his father telling him that "we must lend ourselves to enjoy the arts" and boy, this was art!

With the night sky now above him, Ichi rested in his hammock and took one last look toward the heavens and all the beautiful bright and shining stars. He gave a sigh of relief as he anticipated the excitement for what lay ahead in his journey to Mountain Temple.

Despite the chirping of the frogs, the howling of the wolves, the buzzing of the fireflies growing louder and louder, it all seemed like a choir singing a lullaby, as Ichi quickly fell asleep.

Early, the next morning, Ichi woke up to the sound of hummingbirds zooming around his head in their search for food. "Whoa, look at these guys! They fly so fast!" Ichi exclaimed, as he watched several of them go from flower to flower.

It was a bright and sunny morning as Ichi strapped on his backpack and secured his sword. He then adjusted his helmet, as he continued his journey to Mountain Temple.

Ichi's path took him up a tall mountain, from which he could see the entire valley.

"Wow, this is amazing! There seems to be a small village over there. It must be Shang Na Village," Ichi said to himself, as he took out his map.

"Let's see," he continued, "according to this map, Shang Na Village is located right next to Nabe River."

He guided his finger down the map, found the river and, lo and behold, there was the village!

"Ah, yes! That's Shang Na Village alright! According to these directions, I will make it there by this afternoon. But because I got up extra early, I'll make it there a little sooner so I can shop for some peanuts," added Ichi.

"I'm running a little low on my peanuts, but I think they will last until I get to Shang Na Village," said Ichi to himself. "Perhaps they will have some different types of peanuts there! Maybe they will have those chocolate covered peanuts I've heard so much about!"

Shang Na Village

Within five hours, he had arrived at the village, just slightly ahead of schedule. According to Sifu's instructions, he would be staying in Shang Na Village for two days.

"Wow, this is an amazing town, much bigger than I thought," Ichi said to himself, "The Dragon Inn, on the far side of the town, that's where I am supposed to be staying for a couple of days. I'm looking forwarding to sleeping in a nice and cozy place," as Ichi checked into his room and put his backpack on the bed and headed out the door to explore the marketplace.

As he strolled through the vendor booths, he noticed a lot of people gathering in the streets. It just so happened that it was festival time in Shang Na Village, so everyone was taking part singing and dancing throughout the village.

Although Ichi was not a very good dancer in the slightest, he still loved to dance and happily joined in on the festivities. There were all kinds of different foods, a variety of interesting costumes and lots and lots of great music.

Called the "Festival of Life," Ichi had never witnessed this much enthusiasm before and he was soon caught up with great emotion.

The hiking and the dancing took their toll on Ichi. He ran out of breath in just the first five dances! To catch his breath, he decided to partake in all the great delicacies that were prepared just for the event.

"Hmmm, this is wonderful," Ichi exclaimed as he filled his plate with some interesting and exotic cultural foods. But, it wasn't long until Ichi was back on the floor again, dancing up a storm!

Although the festival had ended, Ichi enjoyed the second day exploring the village, meeting the townsfolk and stocking up on supplies. He was especially glad to find the chocolate-covered peanuts he had heard so much about.

Even though Ichi and Kekoa were in the same village, Sifu adjusted their time frames so that they wouldn't meet up until later on.

An Unexpected Encounter

Packing up his gear, Ichi walked to the end of town, where he met up with a divided pathway. Ichi then took out his map to determine which route he should take.

"Okay, the pathway on the right is going in the direction of the river and that's the one I'm supposed to take," Ichi deduced - and for about two and a half miles he did. Then, the path veered off back into the forest. There were tall, beautiful trees that gave plenty of shade for his trip. According to the map, the pathways were supposed to join together just ahead.

Ichi then noticed from a distance, on the adjoining path, an old woman was driving a one-horse cart. She was going very slow. The cart was so old, it didn't seem possible it was still operating!

In the distance, there was Kekoa walking!

Ichi was so excited to see her, he yelled out her name! But, she was too far away to hear him.

"Aiyaah!" cried out the old woman, as her cart started to wobble ferociously.

All of a sudden, he saw Kekoa drop her backpack and run like the wind toward the old woman. "Something's wrong," said Ichi.

It was then that he saw that the cart had lost a wheel! So, like Kekoa, Ichi dropped his pack and ran across the trail toward the woman as fast as his little feet could take him!

The horse started kicking even more as the cart shook violently, both to the left and the right! The old woman dropped the reins, as she got knocked from one side to the other.

Ichi saw that Kekoa had reached the old woman in time and saved her from falling. However, the cart started to lean over too far in their direction and was about to fall on top of them!

As quickly as he was able, Ichi reached out as far as he could and pulled the cart back. "Whoa, horsey!" said Ichi from the other side of the cart.

"Hey, thanks! You came just in time!" exclaimed Kekoa, with a surprised look on her face, "It was like it was meant to be."

"You said it!" replied Ichi, "You must be Kekoa."

"And you must be Ichi," said Kekoa.

"Well thank you again, young lady, and thank you, young gentleman," said the old lady. "I don't know what I would have done if you two hadn't come along like you did!"

"Now, you rest right here," said Ichi as he patted a nearby tree stump as Kekoa went to retrieve her backpack and Ichi did the same when she returned so the old woman wouldn't be left alone.

"Okay! Ichi, let's see if we can fix this old cart!" challenged Kekoa.

Kekoa leaned down and picked up the wheel from the ground. Ichi headed into the forest, where he retrieved a long, thick and sturdy stick, perfect for holding up the cart long enough to slip the wheel back on.

With a rock and some makeshift tools, they reattached the wheel. Then, off the three of them went!

The Hidden Warrior

"You know, my home is not far from here. Not far at all. Would you youngin's mind traveling with me a bit?" asked the old woman.

"Sure. How far is your home?" questioned Kekoa.

"Very close. Yes. Very close," said the old woman, who added, "By the way, everyone calls me Grandma T."

About an hour later, they stopped for a rest. "A bumpy ride, eh dearies? Now, as I said, my home is just up the road a bit. Right around the next bend."

Two more hours later, they stopped and ate together. Grandma T told them some stories about the surrounding villages and the battles they went through when she was young.

"Oh yes, dearies, it was a time of war and many fierce battles! It was a dark time in the history for our village," remembered Grandma T.

"Grandma T, I heard back then there was this great warrior. She was called Tina Timura, the greatest of them all. They said she led the army that saved the nation of Siulum. She became a real legend and kept everyone safe," declared Kekoa.

"Right you are honey! She was the greatest and most cunning warrior of all time, so I hear! It has been said that she could take on twenty of the enemy at a time and beat them all! She was indeed a legend...but let's talk more on the road shall we?" urged Grandma T, as they all got back up on the cart and continued their expedition.

"How far did you say your home was Grandma T?" queried Ichi.

"Oh, we are really close," she replied back. "Very close."

As they continued their adventure deep into the forest, Grandma T recalled more stories of the old war and how the four villages had fought together to defend the Siulum nation.

Three hours later, just as nightfall began, a lovely set of cottages lay just in front of them. "There it is, dearies! I told you it was just a wee bit ahead of us. Aren't they all grand? I was born in this very spot. Just a stone's throw away from the village," reported Grandma T.

"A long throw, Grandma T," mentioned Ichi, with a smile on his face.

"Ha, ha," laughed Kekoa.

"Hey, I got so caught up in our conversation, I forgot to look at our map," added Kekoa, as they pulled out their maps to compare. "We must be really far off the trail by now."

At that moment, they arrived at Grandma T's front door. They looked up and gazed upon a unique family crest that looked like an ancient shield.

"Wow! That is a very cool looking family crest! It's a warriors crest I believe. Am I right?" asked Ichi.

"Well yes it is! How nice of you to notice," stated Grandma T.

"Hey, Ichi, look at this map," urged Kekoa.

"What? Oh yeah! How far off are we?" asked Ichi.

"It says here, we are to stay at the home of Tina Timura! It lists her as the greatest warrior of all time, the leader of the nation and savior of the community!"

"Hey, that's who we were talking about!" exclaimed Ichi. "That's going to be exciting, meeting her!"

"She will tell us stories of her battles! She will also teach us the basics of the art of Chi Kung - internal breathing!" Kekoa blurted, as she looked at the map and noticed a family crest over their intended destination.

They both looked up and also recognized that the very same family crest was on the doorway!

"Hey, wait a minute! Grandma T, are you the great warrior? Are you Tina Timura?" wondered Kekoa.

"Yep, that's me, but Grandma T is just fine," she replied.

"You are too funny! You knew it all along and didn't tell us," laughed Ichi.

"Now what fun would that be dearie," asked a laughing Grandma T, "but here we are!"

You are both welcome to my humble home! Put your stuff down! We got a whole bunch more talking to do - and some things that Sifu asked me to show you."

Book One: The Adventures of Ichi and His Friends

Shinji

Shinji and Lalo are the two youngest of all the warriors. Without question, Shinji was the most excited to go on the excursion to Mountain Temple. He was anxious, inquisitive and full of energy.

Shinji was Ichi's younger cousin.

Shinji was the son of Fumio and Takemi.

Shinji's father, Fumio, is an actual brother to Toshi. They were and continue to be very close. Toshi is Ichi's father.

Shinji's mother, Takemi, grew up with her best friend Rumiko. Rumiko got married to Toshi, so now they are sisters-in-law. So, Rumiko is Shinji's aunt.

Shinji's village practiced a very traditional art form called Shinobi, which is based on the "art of the shadow". They are able to maneuver without being seen, as well as carry some of the coolest gadgets known to man!

Because he was still so young, Shinji had only learned the fun parts of the art, such as the smokescreen and a few simple throwing gadgets. He needed a few more years to grow and appreciate the true nature of it.

Unfortunately, Shinji had a tendency to rush into a situation without thinking, so he needed to learn patience and how to work as a team player.

Although he is not as skilled in the martial arts as the others, he had the strongest heart and a will that wouldn't allow him to give up, no matter what.

He loved to laugh and tried to make everything fun.

He really enjoyed hanging with his cousin, Ichi. He looked up to him and respected him and loved to follow him around and he always listened to his advice.

Shinji was still a little kid with a lot of growing up to do, but with Sifu, he would eventually learn patience and how to appreciate things.

The Art of Disappearance

"Okay class. Now pay close attention as I take this small, little device and make so much smoke you won't even be able to see me as I disappear," pointed out Sensei Kubota.

"Oh, this is going to be so much fun, Sensei! Can I do it? Can I?" asked Shinji, with great enthusiasm as he raised his hand so high, he could almost touch the ceiling!

"Shinji, you have to let the teacher show you how it's done first," said Sensei.

"Oh, yeah," remarked Shinji, as the class started to laugh at him and he joined them.

"The class for this semester is called 'The Art of Disappearance.' It is about being able to vanish in an instant," commented the instructor. "The art of disappearing can be done in many ways. In this case, these really handy smoke bombs do the trick. Each warrior will carry about six devices with them."

"Hopefully, that will be enough! However, not only will you learn how to use them like a professional, you will also learn how to build your own."

"Really?!" the class said in unison, with excitement on their faces.

"Yes, you will! Even you, Shinji," said Sensei, with laughter in his voice. "Now watch closely."

With his right hand Sensei Kubota lifted up the smoke bomb and - in what seemed like a blur - the smoke bomb hit the ground and erupted like a volcano of smoke!

The students reacted with a big, amazed "Whoa!"

in unison. Sensei Kubota was nowhere to be found!

Within seconds, Sensei lept across the room and out of sight. However, the students were so mesmerized by the smoke bomb, they didn't notice the teacher had disappeared!

Every student leaned forward in their chair to see. However, Shinji leaned a little too far and actually fell off the desk. But with all the excitement, no one noticed and no one cared.

"Would you look at that!" exclaimed Shinji, as he ran up close to see the smoke bomb now exploded. Immediately, the whole class followed him as they examined the remnants of the bomb.

"Hey, class, I'm over here!" yelled out Sensei, now on the other side of the room and waving to get his students' attention. "The point of the smoke bomb is to conceal your escape with smoke. If you would all look this way, instead of being occupied by the exploded bomb, you can see that it worked! I was able to put up a smokescreen as I quickly moved away."

"Ah, yes! I see, Sensei," nodded Shinji as he and the class still admired the remnants of the smoke bomb. "Can we try it now?" he excitedly asked, as he looked at Sensei Kubota.

"Well, there are 20 smoke bombs here in this box, one for each of us. If we go one at a time..." Sensei started to explain, but in less than two seconds, the whole class ran up and grabbed their smoke bomb and at the same time, threw them on the ground to ignite them.

"BOOM! BOOM! BOOM!" the smoke bombs had filled the room with so much smoke, it was nearly impossible for the students to see each other.

"That was great! Wow! Yeah! Let's do it again," yelled out the students with glee.

"Okay! Okay! Yes, it was fun. But now we have nothing to work with! So, for the next hour, you are all going to learn how to make these amazing smoke bombs. We are also all going to learn how to ignite them and how to use them to escape, isn't that right class?" commanded Sensei.

"Yes, escape Sensei," the class replied in unison.

"You can use just ordinary items to make them. You just have to be careful," challenged Sensei. "Shinji, your journey is coming up and we are all so proud of you. Make sure you learn this well! You never know when it can come in handy."

The Trip Ahead

"Shinji, you are stuffing your face with so much food that one would think you were traveling across the desert," said Shinji's mother, Takemi, with a funny grin on her face.

"I can't help it mom," Shinji uttered with a mouthful of eggs. "Who knows when I will find something to eat out there in the wilderness. It may be days - even weeks! - out there in the freezing cold and the blazing heat."

"Honey, you won't be on the trail for at least five more hours. In fact, you will be eating lunch before you go," reminded Takemi. "You know, you will be going through many villages along the way where you can get something to eat."

"Oh, that's right, I forgot," realized Shinji as he continued to stuff more eggs into his cheeks.

"Shinji," said his father Fumio. "Have you packed enough clothes in your backpack?"

"Yep, papa, I did it all last night," replied Shinji, as he chugged down the last of the milk. "Aah!"

"You know, you can never have enough underwear," pointed out Takemi as she put in a few extra pairs of briefs in Shinji's bag.

"Aw mom," fretted Shinji, "I can wear the same underwear for at least a week."

Takemi had an embarrassed look on her face, "Don't you dare, young man!" she said. "Promise me you will change every day."

"Okay," Shinji agreed, "I will."

Fumio leaned over to Shinji and whispered, "Make sure you don't forget any of these," as he placed some smoke bombs in his backpack.

"I can take those?" wondered Shinji, who was suddenly so full of excitement that a smile spread across his face.

"Oh, sure," exclaimed his father, with a slight bit of hesitation in his voice, "but I think we also need to add some throwing stars and some rope."

"Some darts, too! I can't forget the darts," snapped Shinji, as he reached for them on the shelf.

"Yes, and take the black darts. You can't see them at night! You are welcome to take my favorite sword as well!" revealed Fumio.

"Yeah! Yeah! Yeah! Can't see them at night! Good idea!" exclaimed Shinji.

"Oh you two, you're like two kids in a candy store," remarked Takemi, who had her hands on her hips. "You know, you're not going to war! You are going to study at Mountain Temple."

"But you never know," remarked Fumio.

"Right, you never know when they can come in handy! Maybe a ferocious creature comes out of the jungle, like a bear or a lion or a gorilla and I need a smokescreen to get away!" suggested Shinji.

"That's true," added Fumio, "The kid has a point. Here, take my personal stash of smoke bombs too. You can never have too many."

"There are no bears or lions or gorillas in Siulum. Shinji, I want you to mind your cousin Ichi, instructed his mom, Takemi. "I am so glad he waited two years for you to be old enough so that you could be together! Your Aunt Rumiko brought up a really wonderful boy! So be sure to always ask him for guidance."

"Your Auntie Rumiko and I have always been very close," noted Takemi. "As you know, she and I grew up together. In fact, she's closer to me than my own sister. We wanted our children to be as close as we were and I am so glad you and Ichi are just like the two of us."

"Didn't Ichi leave for Mountain Temple already," asked Shinji.

"Right, earlier today. You will meet up with Lalo first and you two will travel together. This way you two will get to know each other," added his father.

"I hope Lalo's a fun kid," wondered Shinji.

"He's actually the same age as you, so you should have a few things in common," noted his father.

"Lalo comes from a royal family. He's the grandson of a King, so he's a Prince. It will be your job to help him fit in with everyone. So, I'm depending on you to make him feel welcome," explained his mom.

"Hey, how do you know so much about Lalo," queried Shinji.

"Well, all the parents of all those traveling to Mountain Temple have met together for the past year. The goal has been preparing us to be okay with our children going to the temple. We have met with Sifu many times and discussed the needs of our village," divulged Takemi.

"You met Sifu! Whoa! What's he like? Is he nice, is he really strict? Tell me! Tell me! Tell me!" bubbled Shinji, as his face lit up with anxiousness.

"Ah, that's for you to find out," pointed out his father. "This is a big step for you and we have done our best by meeting with Sifu to ensure each one of you kids will have a wonderful time there."

"That reminds me, I think I will pack some of these new cherry-flavored peanuts for Cousin Ichi. You know how he can't resist peanuts," laughed Shinji.

"Hahaha, he takes after your auntie. She also enjoys peanuts but Ichi really loves them," beamed his mother.

"Will you look at the time," exclaimed Shinji. "It's getting close to lunchtime."

"Honestly Shinji, I don't know where you put all that food. You just finished breakfast a little while ago," his mother sighed.

"I'm a growing boy so I need my nourishment,"

explained Shinji, as he patted his stomach.

A short time after lunch, Fumio began to strap on Shinji's backpack. "Hold still, Shinji! Let me get your pack fully secured."

Fumio whispered, "Don't tell your mother, but I've attached a small, separate pack. It contains some of my favorite throwing stars!"

"No worries, papa," whispered Shinji, as he hid the pack. "Hey, where's the map? I had it here somewhere."

"Right here, young man!" exclaimed Takemi as she pulled it out of his backpack.

"Ha, ha, I forgot I packed it," Shinji laughed, as he unfolded the map to take a last look at the trail.

"Okay honey, look here," Takemi advised her son, "You are going to take this trail and you will travel for quite some time and stop at a Kawa Village along the way. You can get something to eat and you can stay there for the night."

"Yep," exclaimed Shinji. "That looks right. Later I'll hook up with Lalo. Then, I'll catch up to Ichi and Kekoa?"

"Right," said his father. "So, are you ready for this great adventure son?"

"I'm ready," said Shinji, "but will you walk with me for the first mile?"

"Of course we will," replied his mom. They began their walk together for about a mile or so and then stopped.

"Well, I think I'm good from here," said Shinji.

His father commented, "How do you feel my

son?"

"Papa, this is one of the most exciting days of my life and I am so happy my parents can share even just the first mile of it with me. I'm as ready as I will ever be," revealed Shinji.

They both gave Shinji a big hug, which lasted about two minutes. His mom gave him an extra two kisses on the cheek, as Shinji took his first step into a whole new world.

Shinji's Journey Begins

Because Shinji and Lalo were the youngest of the group, Sifu had placed a few monks and villagers to walk with them along their path. Sifu had assured both of their parents that each of them would not be completely alone. In other words, they were looked after throughout their entire journey.

Knowing that Shinji was more excited and - of course - more impatient than the rest, Sifu believed that he might ignore the path he created for him and arrive at Mountain Temple too early. So, Sifu put a few obstacles in his way to slow him down a bit.

"Hello, young man," remarked an elderly villager who just happened to be going in the same direction as Shinji, "Where might you be going?"

"I'm on a journey, sir," replied Shinji as he bowed to the old man.

"What's that you say? It's your birthday! Well, happy birthday, sonny," the old man said with a smile on his face.

"No, I'm on a journey," he stated a little louder.

"A journey? How marvelous! From the looks of things, this must be your first," replied the villager.

"Yes, how did you know?" wondered Shinji.

"Oh, when you get to be my age, sonny boy, you will be on many journeys," replied the villager. "In fact, you remind me of myself when I went on my first journey. Back then, I could run like the wind! But my feet ain't what she used to be!"

Just then, the villager slightly stumbled on a rock and Shinji grabbed his arm before the villager lost his balance. "Oh, thank you sonny! My balance ain't what she used to be either," proclaimed the villager, as he smiled and rubbed his chin back and forth.

"As I was saying, my first and most memorable adventure was traveling to Mountain Temple!"

"Mountain Temple?" exclaimed Shinji, with a look of excitement on his face.

"Yes. That was the first of many adventures," recalled the villager.

"This here satchel is getting a little heavy for an old man like me, said the villager. "You're a strong lad! You can carry this for an old man, yes? You know my strength, she just ain't what she used to be."

"Sure, no problem," Shinji said, as he put the satchel on his right shoulder and helped to balance the man with his arm. "May I ask your name, sir?"

"My name is Masao. I went to Mountain Temple... ooh, about 70 years ago. That was before you were born. You're not 70 years old are you?"

"No Uncle Masao," replied Shinji.

"Well, as I was saying, it was there that I met this

lovely girl. Her name was Mamiko. Cutest thing you ever saw!"

"She always wore a little flower in her hair. Years later, we married. In fact, here she comes now," Masao waved to his wife, who happened to be wearing a bright yellow flower in her hair."

"Honey, this young man is going to our old school, Mountain Temple!" Masao informed his wife.

"Oh, how wonderful. What is your name young man?" asked Mamiko.

"It's Shinji, Auntie Mamiko. It's a pleasure to meet you," as he bowed to both of them in respect.

"Oh, look at you!" declared Mamiko. "So courteous, carrying my husband's satchel for him. Such a nice boy. Here, let me balance you out and I'll put my bag on your other arm," as she lifted her satchel and put it on his other shoulder.

"There, now that's better! Thank you child, now you are balanced out nicely," commented Mamiko.

Shinji's body went down just a little bit from the weight of the two bags.

"This feels like a big bag of some heavy rocks," Shinji expressed.

Walking much slower, with all the weight on him, Shinji said with a slightly heavy breath, "So you also went to Mountain Temple! Tell me about it!"

"Well, let me see. I recall learning all sorts of things," commented Mamiko. "From music and poetry, to history and martial arts. I learned how to invent new and exciting things to help my village. You will have a wonderful time and best of all, you will make life-long friends! One of them - right here - was meeting my future husband, Masao."

"Whew! Carrying all these bags is a lot of work!" exclaimed Shinji, as he brushed the sweat from his brow. "Let me get out my map and see where I'm at - and how far it is to Kawa Village!" as they sat upon a nearby stump to rest.

Shinji stretched the map across a flat rock and all three of them looked at it. Mamiko pointed out, "Look here! Masao, this is where you grew up."

"Yes, that's right. Look over here honey. Remember this place? This is where we had our first official date, right there at Fang Shiyu's restaurant," added Masao, with pride in his voice because he had remembered.

"No dearest, you are mistaken!" Mamiko asserted. "We had our first date at Chiba restaurant."

Mamiko, with her arms now crossed, started reminding him of the specific details. "I remember you had the teriyaki chicken and I had the fish."

"You are probably right, darling," said Masao. Masao then leaned over to Shinji and said on the outside of his mouth, "Get used to that line, sonny."

Studying the map a little longer, Shinji continued, "Okay, well, let's see where we are now. Where's Kawa Village? Look, there it is! It's about an hour away. Cool!"

After several more miles, the road divided into two different directions.

"Well young man, this is where we part!" Masao said to Shinji. "We're going this way home. It was so kind of you to help us."

"It was my pleasure!" Shinji stated. "Thank you

for telling me about Mountain Temple. Please have a safe journey home," said Shinji. "Here are your bags, Uncle Masao and Auntie Mamiko."

"Here, let me help you with that," mentioned Mamiko. "I picked up some great rocks for my rock collection."

"Huh? I thought they were rocks!" laughed Shinji, as he waved goodbye to the couple and headed toward Kawa Village.

Because of all the weight of the many bags he was carrying, Shinji was completely exhausted and just as Sifu had planned, he was now walking a little slower.

Shinji leaned over to take a few sips of water from a nearby cool stream as he took off his shoes to relax.

Since parting with Masao and Mamiko, Shinji ran into several villagers along the trail. Many were kind enough to offer him some snacks - and Shinji was happy to try them all!

As Shinji began to cross over a small bridge, he stopped at the center and threw a few crumbs to the fish. He laughed as they splashed water on him and as they scurried to get some food.

Just as night was about to fall, Shinji arrived at Kawa Village and was completely exhausted. According to the map, he was supposed to stay at the home of Louie Sato, which was the fourth home on the right side of the village.

"There it is!" Shinji exclaimed, as he walked up to the door and knocked. "KNOCK, KNOCK, KNOCK! Is this the Louie Sato family residence?" he asked. "Ah, young Shinji! Welcome! We have been expecting you.

Sifu has prepared us for your visit. Please do come in," requested Louie Sato. "Please call me Uncle Louie. You will be staying with us for two days."

"Uncle Louie," said Shinji as he bowed, took off his shoes and walked into the house. "It is my honor to be here."

"You must be tired from your journey. You can rest right here in this room," Louie offered.

"Oh, yes, I'm so tired I could barely keep my eyes open," Shinji exclaimed, while putting down his pack. He then sat down on the bed.

"The family and I are going to town for the farmer's market, where they will have an assortment of food, snacks and great things to munch on!" Louie noted enthusiastically, as they headed toward the door.

"What?! Snacks! My rest can wait! Lead the way Uncle Louie! Lead the way!" Shinji bellowed as he suddenly had the energy to jump to his feet and head out the door!

The Farmer's Market

The Farmer's Market is a very exciting place at Kawa Village. Every month, at least 20 of the local farmers set up little food stands in the village square. From fresh foods to delicious sweets, there is something for everyone to enjoy.

"Wow! Will you look at this?! I've never seen so many different things to eat! I just don't know where to start," declared Shinji.

"Just take your time and sample each one and pick your favorites," announced Louie, "My treat, young man!"

"Thank you, Uncle Louie!" Shinji yelled, before he excitedly ran to each booth, tasting every delicacy.

Touring the Town

The next morning, Shinji woke up and struggled to get out of bed. Patting his tummy, he joked, "I think I ate the entire village."

"Shinji, during your time here, we have planned a full day for you," remarked Louie. "First, we will go to the town's museum. We have arranged a special tour by the museum curator, Mr. Matsuda, so that you can learn all about us."

"That sounds great. I'm very excited," Shinji replied, as he laced up his shoes.

"Right after that, we are going to Mayor Abesamis' house for a BBQ lunch," said Louie, as he was helping get Shinji's things together.

"I think my tummy should be empty by then," laughed Shinji.

Altogether, he spent two days at Kawa Village. It was a rare treat for Shinji.

Being so young, he hadn't traveled much. So, spending time there was a very fun and educational experience for him.

"Thank you so much," Shinji responded, as he bowed and waved goodbye to the Louie family, while he re-started his journey into the forest.

About two hours into his quest, he heard the sounds of the river just ahead.

Just a few moments later, the pathway led Shinji

to continue his journey along the river bank.

All of a sudden, he heard someone yell out from the river behind him.

Tragedy at Ti Lung River

"Help me! Help me!" yelled out the boatman to Shinji as he saw him walking along the river. "I hit a rock and many of my bags fell off and are now floating down the river! I need help getting them back!"

Shinji saw about 25 bags floating toward him as he yelled back, "I'm on my way!"

Grabbing a rope from his backpack, Shinji made a lasso and whirled it around his head three times. He then snatched the first bag and brought it to the shore.

Again and again, Shinji threw out his rope to lasso the bags. He wasn't successful every time, but he wouldn't give up trying.

As time went on, the bags were starting to spread further apart and go past him. Shinji saw a small boat by the shore and he leaped in and paddled toward the bags. Again, he lassoed another bag, but his efforts weren't enough as the bags were getting too far out of reach.

All of sudden, Shinji saw another rope glide across the sky like a bird in flight.

It landed right on one of the floating bags and was dragged to shore. Shinji smiled because he saw someone just up the river a bit, throwing out a lasso. Together, they captured all the bags from the river.

Shinji then threw a rope to the boatman as they both headed to shore.

"Now this can only be the work of one man," exclaimed Shinji. "The amazing Lalo, I presume!"

Lalo took off his cap as if to bow and laughed as he helped pull them both to shore. "Right you are, Shinji!" Lalo bellowed. "Right you are!"

"Whew!" replied the boatman, "How fortunate I am that you two youngsters came along!"

"Otherwise, all my food and supplies would have washed down the river!"

"Food? What kind of food?" wondered Shinji, with much eagerness in his voice.

"Yeah, what kind of food," added Lalo, as he looked at all the bags with a gaze in his eyes.

"Well, let me see. This bag has some nuts and this one has some rice and this one has some dried fruits," replied the boatman. "Just for helping me out, you two can have all you want."

"Yeah!!!" cheered Lalo and Shinji in unison, as they both quickly reached in and grabbed a few nuts from the bags.

"Thank you sir," said Shinji. "Thank you," added Lalo. "We are very grateful for your generosity."

"Least I can do to thank you boys," claimed the boatman, as he and the boys started putting the bags on the boat and tying them securely. "Now, where are you two youngsters headed?"

"They are having a big community cookout and we're supposed to be a couple of chefs," explained Lalo as he took out his map. "According to our trail, we are supposed to head toward Iwa Village and to get there, we need to hitch a ride with a boatman named Captain Goyo."

"Well, bust my britches! That's what this here food and supplies are for!" exclaimed the boatman. "I'm Captain Goyo and I'm going way down river to Iwa Village to feed some of the needy there with this food! I heard there are a bunch of new cooks that will be joining us. Might that be you?"

"Yep, that's us. We'll be meeting with two more along the way!" explained Shinji.

"Well then, hop along young fellas and let's head to Iwa Village! We have a lot of stops along the way to pick up more food and supplies. It should take us a couple of days to get there, so make yourself a cozy place to relax and enjoy the trip!" exclaimed Captain Goyo.

Lalo

Lalo and Shinji were the most compatible of the young adventurers. Both the same age, they were fast and agile and somehow, they always seemed to get in some kind of trouble together.

Since they were both always the center of attention, they would continually try to outdo each other in little competitions, such as who ate more pasta than the other, who was able to finish their chores faster or who did their martial arts better.

The Meiyo Village was Lalo's hometown. In fact, it is more commonly referred to as the Meiyo Kingdom. It is located at the edge of the forest and is double the size of all three villages combined.

The Kingdom of Meiyo was ruled by a monarchy, which included a king and queen, prince and princess, a military and a household full of servants.

Lalo's family came from a long line of warriors. In fact, Lalo was the grandson of the great King Fari Roiles and Queen Lori Roiles and son of Prince Zafu and Princess Cynthia. As the eldest child, Lalo will eventually serve as the King of Meiyo.

Lalo was brought up in royal tradition since his birth and servants were there to meet his every need. Lalo, however, considered the servants more like his extended family.

As part of royalty, their meals were especially prepared with every detail, including napkins folded to look like swans, candles and the best utensils of the time.

Although Lalo's manners were a little more proper than the rest of the children traveling to Mountain Temple, when he hung around Shinji, he tended to forget them all.

Lalo was very skilled in the martial arts and although he was more skilled than Shinji, he always helped him improve.

A Royal Sendoff

"Whew," I'm bushed. "I've never done so much celebrating," exclaimed Lalo as he wiped the sweat from his brow and took a seat on one of the couches.

"Tired already my grandson? The night is still young and I feel like I'm only 18 years old," laughed King Roiles, as he continued to dance even though the music had already stopped. "Bet you didn't think your grandfather still had some life left in him! Haha!"

"Well my son, are you enjoying this farewell celebration week that I have thrown in your honor? Such a fitting way to launch you on your trip to Mountain Temple," said his father, Prince Zafu, as he quenched his thirst with a drink.

"I think there has been too much celebrating, my husband," said Princess Cynthia, with an exhausted look on her face. "I think one day would have been fine."

"One day, that's unheard of," challenged Prince Zafu. "Yes, I agree," replied King Roiles. "One day is not enough for my grandson. Isn't that right Lalo?"

"Right grandfather! It should have been two weeks!" exclaimed Lalo as he stretched out his arms above his head with a big yawn.

For nearly the entire week, Prince Zafu had planned a series of fun events to launch Lalo's odyssey to Mountain Temple. One night featured singing, another a cookout, while yet another was full of sports activities. The final day was topped off with cultural dancing and music.

"Okay you kids, you've got just one hour to rest. Then, we head toward the center of the village where the music and dancing will continue," noted King Roiles.

After what seemed like only a few minutes of rest, the family was awakened by the thumping of the drums. THUMP-PA-THUMP-PA-THUMP! The beat was both loud and catchy, so much so that one couldn't prevent their feet from tapping to the beat!

"Do you hear that sound, Lalo?" asked the King as he danced his way out of the chair with his hands moving from side to side from the beat, "Guess what time it is?"

"No, not now! It feels like we just sat down," expressed Princess Cynthia, who laid comfortably on the couch with a wet towel on her forehead.

"Hahaha! It's celebration time!" exclaimed Prince Zafu, with excitement in his voice. He reached for his wife's hand and tried to assist her off the couch.

"Let's sit this one out and get a little rest," pleaded Princess Cynthia.

"Oh, I think not. This is Lalo's last night of celebration in the streets! You can rest next week," laughed Prince Zafu as he started to dance around the room, pretending like he was holding his wife in his arms.

"Yeah, mom! Let's go out to the festival and dance up a storm," said Lalo with great anticipation.

"Alright, for you my son! Just for you," replied Princess Cynthia.

"C'mon grandmother," yelled out Lalo. "I'm right behind you," said Queen Lori from across the room.

THUMP-PA,THUMP-PA! were the sounds of the music as the whole family headed out the door and to the center of the village, where they found everyone joining in on the final evening of the festival.

You could hear the crowd singing, the people mingling and the smell of barbecue delicacies filling the air. The celebration went deep into the night and after a few hours, the villagers were fast asleep. Amazingly, the town was, once again, as quiet as a mouse.

Lalo Prepares For His Odyssey

"Now let me see," said King Roiles, as he looked at his piece on the game board. He was stroking his chin with his forefinger and thumb, as if his life depended on it. "This is a game of strategy you know," he stated strongly as he moved his piece. "One must evaluate every obstacle ahead of them. Now, let me see."

"Was that your move, grandfather?" smiled Lalo, sitting across from him.

"Now, now, just a moment, I haven't taken my finger off my checker yet."

"Patience, my grandson! Patience is what wins battles, you see! You know, I remember the battle of the archer's way back when I was a young man. Well... we'll leave that for another day," pointed out King Roiles. "This is my move! Yes, this is the one I believe is a good maneuver," as he let go of his red checker very slowly.

"Are you sure, grandfather?" remarked Lalo.

"Ah, yes...wait, wait, let me see," King Roiles stated as he examined his move again, "Yes, this is it! A move fit for a King! Hahaha!"

But just as King Roiles lifted his hand, Lalo took his black marker and hopped over three of King Roiles' checkers and exclaimed "King me grandfather!"

"Oh, my! That was quite clever my lad, quite clever. Looks like you have the upper hand now," exclaimed the King.

"Young Master Lalo, I do believe it's time to get ready," said Thora, the King's head servant.

"Thanks Auntie Thora," remarked Lalo. "Grandfather, we will have to continue this game when I come back home to visit."

"Yes, it will be right here and I think by then, I shall study this game board and I may surprise you with some new moves," pointed out King Roiles.

With the help of Thora, Lalo began to pack his things to prepare for the journey.

"Now we need to make room for some special treats I can munch on along the way," noted Lalo.

"Don't worry, we have plenty of room, Master Lalo," added Thora.

The King walked into Lalo's room and helped him pack, as well. "Lalo, my grandson, always remember that family is very important and building relationships with our other villages is building upon that family. For the next several years, you must learn to depend on them as they will depend on you. You understand what I mean?"

"Yes grandfather, I do," nodded Lalo.

"I know you aren't too familiar with the children from the other villages, so this is your opportunity to get to know them! Hopefully, you can become great friends!"

"Mom, I'm supposed to meet with Shinji first, correct?" asked Lalo.

"Yes. Oh, Shinji's mom is so nice. His dad tells me that Shinji loves to use smoke bombs," confessed

Princess Cynthia.

"Oooh, smoke bombs! He sounds very cool," laughed Lalo.

"Be sure you pack some extra underwear! You can never have enough, you know," said his grandmother, Queen Lori, as she took a few pairs from the cabinet and put them in his bag.

"Ah, grandmother," said Lalo.

"Be sure to pack your good ones too," added Queen Lori, as she packed a few more in his bag.

"I'm a little worried about being so far away from everyone," confessed Lalo.

"Oh, don't worry. We will be visiting you all the time and you can come home for all our special events and even birthdays," added King Roiles, "Don't forget, I plan to beat you at checkers when you return!"

Since Lalo's village is the furthest from Mountain Temple, Lalo's journey will be by both foot and by cart, in order to catch up with the rest of the gang. Because Lalo is young like Shinji, Sifu has prepared a special adventure so that the monks and the villagers can watch over him most of the way.

"According to the map Sifu gave us, you will first walk the trail for about three hours and you will eventually reach a trading post. There, you will hop aboard a travel cart and ride with several of the other villagers for about five or six hours," explained his father, Prince Zafu.

"Don't I get to eat?" questioned Lalo.

"Yes, they will stop many times along the way for you to eat, so don't worry," confirmed the Prince.

Book One: The Adventures of Ichi and His Friends

"Whew! Don't want to miss lunch," laughed Lalo.

"Toward the evening, you will reach Waimea Village. You will be staying at the home of Grandma Oda. She will teach you the ways of her people and introduce you to the fun art of surfing. Boy, I haven't surfed in a long time! Maybe I should join you," remarked Prince Zafu, holding his arms out as if he was riding a surfboard.

"That is the home of Kekoa's grandmother. You will spend a couple of days there. Sifu wants you to get to know Kekoa's people," explained his mom, Princess Cynthia.

"Oooh! That sounds neat! I heard that Waimea Village has best food in all of Siulum and I can't wait to try some of those spicy dishes! Mmmm! Mmmm!" confessed Lalo.

"Now remember, there will be no one to pick up after you. You will be like everyone else, so do your best to get along with everyone," said Princess Cynthia."

"I will, mom," said Lalo.

After everyone helped Lalo to pack, they headed out to the pathway that Sifu had prepared for him.

A Journey Begins

"Well my son, here we are - at the beginning of your trail. Your grandfather said he needs some exercise, so he will walk with you for a little bit further," commented Prince Zafu. "Now give me a big hug. We will miss you but we will see you shortly."

Prince Zafu and Princess Cynthia both gave Lalo a big, crushing embrace.

"Mom! Dad! You are squeezing the air out of me!"

110

exclaimed Lalo, with his arms down on his side, feeling as he's like a sandwich being swished at both ends.

Queen Lori then joined in to squish him even more.

"Bye, everyone! I will see you all in a few weeks at the open house," waved Lalo, as he and King Roiles departed together.

King Roiles and Lalo walked together for the next two hours enjoying each other's company. The King and Lalo have been very close, even closer than Lalo's own father. Lalo admired his grandfather so it was only fitting that they should travel the first couple of miles together.

"Ah, as I promised you, two miles and here we are," pointed out the King. "I know this because when I was your age, I used to run to this big rock right here. This rock is exactly two miles from the kingdom."

"Really, is that true?" said Lalo with his eyes widened just a bit further because of his excitement.

"Come with me," as King Roiles took Lalo to the top of a large rock and pointed to some writing there. "Look right here. See these names? For the past hundred years or so, we have had a little, sort of, tradition," as the King brushes the dirt off the names. "This first name is your great, great grandfather's name Prado Roiles. Under him is your great grandfather - my father - Gene Roiles."

"Next is my name, Fari, and under me is your father's name - my son - Zafu."

Lalo looked closely as he helped to dust off the rock a little more, "Wow, grandfather, that is so cool."

The King reached into his pocket and pulled out a writing instrument. "And now, my grandson, it is your turn," as he wrote the name, Lalo Roiles on the big rock.

The Ohana Festival

It had been two full hours since Lalo said his final goodbye to his grandfather. There was an abundance of townfolk along the pathway as Lalo spent a few moments greeting each of them.

Just a short time later, he saw a small trading post just ahead. An elderly man who seemed to have a trail of dust following him, walked up to Lalo and said, "Ah, young feller, if your name is Lalo, we've been waiting for you. My name is Araki Maru."

Araki was an interesting man. He had stunning dark hair and a pair of dark glasses, a long leather jacket and a black, weathered hat. He stood in front of a four horse-drawn trailer cart fitted with a large, brown canopy for shade across the top. It was an open-aired transport that was big enough for twelve to sixteen passengers.

"Hop aboard young man, we saved a seat for you right here with the others," suggested Araki, as he opened the back gate and patted on one of the seats that were available.

"Thank you, Uncle Araki," Lalo replied, as he stepped up into the cart and put down his gear. Then, with a sigh of relief, he sat on a nice, wide and slightly padded seat.

"Giddyup!" shouted out Araki, as the horses began their slow trek down the trail.

"Oh this is so exciting!" remarked Lalo as he extended his hand and greeted each of the other passengers. "My name is Lalo and I'm on my way to Waimea

Village. Have you ever been there?" he asked one of the passengers, a mother with two children. She was wearing a very flowery summer-style dress with a white flower in her hair. She was also carrying a uniquely designed, wooden basket and a leather drinking pouch.

"Yes, that is our home. My name is Lelani. You will love it there," as she reached down into her basket, "We have some extra food. Would you like some? This is a special sweet treat called pandulce. It's made of sugar and bread. I made it myself, but I made a few too many and I don't want them to spoil! Please, try some."

"Boy would I!" remarked Lalo, as he took his first bite, "Wow! This is fantastic! Just fantastic! I've never tasted anything like this! It's so delicious!"

With a slightly embarrassed look on her face, Lelani responded, "Oh, you are just saying that! My cooking isn't that great."

Then, with crumbs all across his mouth, Lalo asked, "Where can I find more of this?"

"You can get some really great treats at many of the stores in the village!"

"I can't wait to try more when we get there. Thank you so much," exclaimed Lalo as he continued to munch on his new found treat.

"Here, take some water from my pouch to wash it down," remarked Lelani.

"Thank you and this is a nice water pouch," added Lalo.

"I made one just like this for my cousin recently," said Lelani.

Although the trail was bumpy and rocky, and

even though the passengers were tossed slightly back and forth like the waves of the ocean, Lalo had an enjoyable six hours talking with the other passengers. He was so consumed in conversation that someone had to let him know that they were about to reach Waimea Village.

"Is that Waimea Village? Really! I can't believe we are already here. Look over there, it's a beach! Right there!" exclaimed Lalo, as he moved about the cart pointing and trying to look at everything. "Look there! Look there! It's the ocean and people are surfing, just like father said. Look at all the seagulls!"

"Hey, young man! You'll have plenty of time to see everything so let's not fall out of the cart until we stop at the station just down the road," cautioned Araki.

"I can't help it," said Lalo, with an excited smile on his face. "I've just never seen anything like this!"

"Whoa!" Araki said, as he pulled back on the reins and settled the cart to a stop. "Well, here we are! Now, young man, you can run around all you like!"

Lalo stepped off the cart and helped everyone down. He grabbed his backpack and noticed that an elderly woman was waiting to greet him.

"Greetings young Lalo, welcome to my village. I'm so glad you have arrived," said Grandma Oda. "You came at a perfect time, it's the last day of our Ohana Festival where we honor our ancestors and reflect on our families' history."

"It is my honor to meet you Auntie Oda," as Lalo bowed in respect.

"Everyone calls me Grandma Oda."

Grandma Oda's house was just down the road

a bit, literally, right on the beach. "Oh, this is so neat! The beach is your front door, Grandma Oda," exclaimed Lalo.

As they walked into her home, Grandma Oda said, "Now, put your things down over here. You go wash up from the dusty road and we'll go into the village. There we can enjoy the festival and get something good to eat. You can use my granddaughter's room. Even though she doesn't actually live here, I do keep a room for her whenever she wants to spend the night."

After a short while, Lalo walked into the living room all refreshed and ready for the evening. "How do I look, Grandma Oda?" remarked Lalo.

"Ah, you look very handsome. Now, let me add a little flower to your shirt," commented Grandma Oda as she used a pin to affix a bright yellow flower onto his garment. "Ah, there, now you are a part of the family," she said, as Lalo smiled.

Grandma Oda was wearing a very colorful and easy flowing outfit, with a circle of green leaves around her head. "This is part of our traditional headwear. I like tradition so I enjoy wearing it. Besides looking really awesome, it keeps our head cool at night," laughed Grandma Oda.

Lalo and Grandma Oda started their walk toward the amphitheater at the town center. Along the way, she pointed out all the unique things about her village.

"Look over there," noted Grandma Oda. "That's Kekoa's favorite surfing area. It's where she catches the biggest waves. And right over there is the best fishing hole. When the water goes back a little, it reveals a nice big pool of water. There are so many fish in there, you can practically grab them with your hands!"

Since the evening was upon them, the town center was now filled with people. It resembled a small stadium, with an oval performance area in the center. There were small tiki flames all around, which gave a traditional style effect.

"Come dear," requested Grandma Oda. "I'm so old, they don't think I can see too far. So, they save these special seats just for me and Kekoa!"

She leaned over to Lalo. Putting her hand slightly cupped over her mouth, so no one was able to hear what they are talking about as Grandma Oda revealed, "I see just fine! But I don't tell them that, otherwise I won't get these great seats!" as she laughed.

The large torches at the center stage were now lit and the drumming began.

THOM! THOM! THOM! went the sound of the drums. Six male warriors appeared as they danced their way across the stage, each of them carrying a shark teeth weapon.

"Grandma, I thought we were going to eat?" Lalo reminded her.

"Ah! This is why I love being the oldest grandma in the entire village. They bring the food to me! Look, here it comes!"

Trays of food were then passed down the aisle to Grandma Oda and her guest.

"Now, you must try everything and I'll tell you about it after you taste it," pointed out Grandma Oda.

"Sounds fine to me," Lalo gladly replied, as he

began tasting the fine delicacies of the village. "Mmm! Mmm! This one is the best Grandma Oda! Oh! Wait! This one is better! No! Wait! This one is much better!"

About an hour into the festivities, a representative from each family was called upon to present their string of shells.

"Grandma Oda, what does all those seashells mean?" whispered Lalo.

"Those shells represent the history of every family in the entire village. Every name for over 400 plus years is listed there," explained Grandma Oda.

"Earlier this week, Kekoa came of the age in which her name has now be placed on one of the shells."

The evening was full of entertainment, tradition and exotic foods. From very powerful martial arts demonstrations to the beautiful dancers who told the story of their culture in just their hand movements.

As his parents and grandparents had told Lalo, this was an opportunity to learn about the other villages.

"Grandma Oda, tonight was amazing! Waimea Village is so awesome!" he confessed.

"Well, I'm glad you had some fun," said Grandma Oda, as she tucked young Lalo into bed. "Sweet dreams Lalo! We have a lot of new and exciting things to explore early tomorrow morning."

"Goodnight grandma, thank you," responded Lalo, as he yawned and went to sleep.

Surf's Up!

It was very early the next morning as Grandma Oda knocked on Lalo's bedroom door. "Are you ready young man?"

"Huh, yeah! I think I'm up. I can't tell!" Lalo said, as he opened one eye with a dazed look on his face.

"Surf's up, dude! It's six in the morning and time to hit the waves!" said Grandma Oda, with a big smile on her face. "I got my board here and you can use Kekoa's right over there! If we get there early enough, we can catch the best waves!" she exclaimed standing there with her arm around her surfboard - like she was holding an old friend.

"Grandma Oda! I'm right behind you! Let's go!" Lalo shouted with excitement, even though he was torn between being half excited and half asleep.

Since Grandma Oda's home was right on the beach, it only took a few steps to get to the sandy area.

For about twenty minutes, she showed Lalo how to prepare the boards, as well as giving him a quick lesson on surfing while still on the beach. Lalo had a little trouble at first balancing himself, but he soon got the hang of it.

"So Lalo, do you think you are ready to try some real surfing on the water?" challenged Grandma Oda, as she picked up her board and started heading toward the ocean.

With an eagerness to hit the waves, Lalo picked up Kekoa's board and exclaimed, "Bet I can beat you to the waves, Grandma Oda!"

"You got it kiddo! Let's hang ten," she said joyfully, as both of them hit the waves together.

It was a full day on the ocean for Grandma Oda and Lalo. From surfing the waves to paddling a canoe to sailing on kayaks to fishing with spears, Lalo got a glimpse into a lifestyle he had never known!

Aware that Shinji and Ichi were cousins, they wouldn't feel alone at Mountain Temple. However, Lalo and Kekoa would be by themselves. So, Sifu arranged for Lalo to learn first-hand about Waimea village so that they would have a few things in common.

Back on the Road

"Mmm! Mmm! Grandma Oda, this breakfast is so good and these cookies are so yummy!" Lalo remarked, "I think I should take a few of these cookies for my journey," he added, as he gobbled down yet another handful.

"I'll wrap a few up so they won't get hard and you can enjoy them later," said Grandma Oda, as she prepared them for his adventure.

A few hours later. "Well young Lalo, it's almost time for you to continue your journey! I hope you had a wonderful time here in my village!" said Grandma Oda, as she helped Lalo pack his bag.

"Oh I did! Thank you, Grandma Oda! I learned a lot!" replied Lalo, with extreme gratitude. "Thank you so much for your wonderful hospitality! I'll be sure to tell Kekoa all about my time here!"

Just then, Grandma Oda pulled out something from the cabinet. "Lalo, Kekoa forgot one of her favorite bracelets. Please, put it in your pack and give it to her when you see her," as she put the bracelet in the palm of his hand and gave him a great big hug.

Cookies! Cookies! Cookies!

Back on his journey, Lalo stopped at a number of eating places along the way. "I wasn't aware there were so many small, little communities out this far the kingdom and everyone is so friendly," Lalo thought to himself.

As he walked along the pathway, he pulled out the map from his back pocket. "Let's see. If I keep going in this direction, I should reach the river by the afternoon."

"Mmm! Mmmm! These cookies that Grandma Oda packed away are out of this world!" Lalo giddily said outside to himself, as he took a moment to rest under a shady tree and gobbled down another cookie.

After a few minutes, an elderly woman walked by and said to him, "Do you mind if I share the shade of this tree with you?"

"Oh, please, have a seat! I will enjoy the company. I have some wonderful cookies! Would you like one?" asked Lalo, as he stood up, bowed to her, as he pulled out another treat from his bag.

"Why, yes, that would be lovely! Thank you! My name is Michie," replied the woman, as she graciously received the cookie and eagerly took a bite from it.

"Now, that is delicious!" remarked Michie in amazement.

"My name is Lalo, Auntie Michie. Do you mind if I ask you a question?"

"Not at all. How can I help?"

Lalo pulled out his map again, unfolded it and held it wide for Michie to see.

"Auntie Michie, are you familiar with this area?

I'm pretty sure I'm following it correctly but I just want to be extra sure."

"Well, let me see," motioned Michie, as she placed a finger on the map. "Yes, I know this area well! Ah, yes! If your plan is to reach Mountain Temple, then yes, you are headed in the right direction! But you've still got a long way to go!"

"That's right!" concurred Lalo. "I'm on my way to Mountain Temple, but it says here in order to get there, I have to go to Ti Lung River and meet up with a boatman," said Lalo.

"Now that would be Captain Goyo! He's my dear friend. I know exactly where you are going!" said Michie excitedly and with renewed confidence. "Look here! If you follow the trail, you will find him around this little stretch here. Captain Goyo has been taking people and supplies up and back down the river for decades!"

"We actually grew up together," Michie continued and started laughing at a memory. "Lalo, you'll like Captain Goyo! He loves to sing, except he can't carry a tune!"

"Come, let me walk with you for spell as I head in that direction."

"Many thanks for your assistance and your company," acknowledged Lalo.

"You can thank me, young man, by telling me all about this journey you are on," Michie added.

So, as they traveled together down the trail toward the river, he did! They had advanced about six miles when they reached a fork in the road. "Well, Lalo, I think this is where we part," Michie informed him.

"If you continue down this path, you will hit the river!" pointed out Michie. "From there, you follow the river and you'll see one of the docking stations just a little ways up, you can't miss it. You can wait there for Captain Goyo's flatboat. Be sure to send my greetings to Goyo!" added Michie.

"Oh yes, I will! Goodbye," Lalo remarked. He then bowed to Michie and continued on the trail.

The Heroes of Ti Lung

It wasn't long before the trail led to the river. "The docking station should be coming into view soon," said Lalo to himself.

After he turned the bend, there was the station. "I must be a little early, no one is here yet. I'll just put them things down and wait for Captain Goyo," said Lalo to himself.

Suddenly, he heard a lot of noise coming down river toward the dock. "Ah, I think I see the boat. Wow, is my timing good or what!" he exclaimed.

However, instead of seeing Captain Goyo at the helm, calmly steering the boat, he saw him running around the boat frantically trying to reach out into the water.

"Over there! There's another one over there!" Captain Goyo was yelling out. "Help anybody!"

"Oh no!" thought Lalo to himself, as he saw the captain's dilemma, "all his supplies were floating away."

Lalo opened up his backpack, pulled out a rope and headed toward the boatman.

As he got closer, he noticed someone out there in

a small canoe doing a fine job lassoing the bags one by one. It must be Shinji, he thought.

Unfortunately, the bags were spreading out in too many directions with an increasing number getting out of the reach of Shinji's lasso.

"Okay," as he ran closer to the flatboat, "Shinji needs some help and here it comes!"

"Wahoo!" Lalo gleefully shouted, as he grabbed his rope and flung a lasso around one of the wayward bags and started to reel it back to the shore. He repeated his maneuver again and again, as he continued to snare bag after bag.

Shinji looked over at Lalo and started laughing. They soon made a fun challenge of their serious chore, by seeing who could lasso the most bags.

"I got another one! Me, too!" yelled out the two young travelers.

That's seven for me!

That's nine for me!

After all the bags were rescued, Lalo threw a rope to Shinji and he threw one to the boatman as he started pulling them both toward the shore.

"Now this can only be the work of one man," exclaimed Shinji. "The amazing Lalo, I presume."

Lalo took off his cap as if to bow and laughed. "Elementary, my dear Shinji! Elementary."

"Whew!" expressed Captain Goyo, "How fortunate I am that you two youngsters came along! Otherwise, all my food and supplies would have washed down the river!"

As the boatman shared his food - as a thank you

to Lalo and Shinji for their rescue - he started to secure the bags back onto his flatboat as he reached the docking station.

Lalo pulled out his map and both Shinji and he followed their path with their fingers. "It says that Iwa Village is our next stop!" exclaimed Shinji.

"Well then, let's get your things on board as we head to Iwa Village," exclaimed Captain Goyo, as he motioned them to bring their backpacks on board.

"There was a villager I met along the way. Her name is Auntie Michie. She said to say hello to you," noted Lalo.

"You met Michie? Ah, Michie, what a wonderful girl! We both grew up together you know? We were like brother and sister! She's a great grandmother now," admitted Captain Goyo proudly. .

"Yes, I believe she mentioned that her grandkid's names are Sara and Goyo," Lalo, recalled, delighted that he remembered, "Hey, that's your name!"

"Right you are, young man! Goyo is named after little ol' me. That was so nice of her. Goyo is the oldest and he always stops by to help me when I have some big loads," added Captain Goyo.

"Well, you young lads and get yourself settled in! I'm going to take care of some business. It's going to be a long but wonderful journey down river to Iwa Village. We'll make a lot of stops at many docking stations along that way and there's plenty of villages we can visit to get something to eat."

Sifu

Sifu was one of the many monks that lived and taught at Mountain Temple.

An expert in many different kinds of martial arts, he also attended some of the most prestigious schools in the world.

Sifu, which was another name for teacher or father, he had been part of a 2,000-year lineage of teachers before him. It had been the duty of the monks at the temple to serve each of the four primary villages by educating a specific number of their young children.

Although most of the monks were considered quite strict in their teaching methods, Sifu acted more like a father figure than someone who just barked out orders.

Sifu believed that the methods used by many of the ancestors were way too excessive. So, he has added his own unique and joyful personality - which at times he used humor as a tool, to teach his students. His unorthodox techniques have paid off for him time and time again by producing some of the best students since Mountain Temple was created.

Sifu was fun, but deadly! He was playful, but wise. He enjoyed spending time with his apprentices and always made their activities a learning experience.

Sifu had a long, white beard, which he stroked periodically. Sifu believed it made him look wiser.

Though skilled in combat fighting and all forms of weaponry, he was always thrilled when someone was able to surprise him with a new technique.

He was always kind and loved nature's creatures of which he had a special bond.

A stairway of water flowed down from the mountains above the temple and would form a large lake where Sifu would often walk along the shore and teach many of his lessons.

Sifu loved to eat! He enjoyed tasting new and exotic foods. He would taste anything offered him, no matter if it was good or bad. With either result, he would always act like it was the most delicious thing he had ever eaten!

Sifu was a man that was well-traveled. For nearly ten years, Sifu had traveled across the world exploring different peoples and cultures. He spent time learning about new ideas and the latest inventions.

Sifu's last name was Kong, but he preferred to just be called Sifu.

Sifu would prepare himself for one year before becoming their teacher. By visiting the parents and the grandparents of each child, he received a better understanding of their gifts and their needs and what each village expected from the Temple.

Book One: The Adventures of Ichi and His Friends

The Journey of Two Warriors

"Whew, this training is tougher than I thought," said an exhausted Kekoa, as she continued standing in a low, sitting position, "I never thought breathing could be so hard."

"You are both warriors. You are both weapons experts, but you need to be more in touch with nature. By having lower stances and proper breathing you draw energy from the earth," stressed Grandma T.

"This is called a horse stance. You bring the energy from the ground, through the body and thrust it out through your palms."

"Place your hands just 12 inches apart, with your palms facing each other. Now, move your body back and forth as you cultivate your energy," motions Grandma T.

"I'm not sure I'm doing it right Grandma T," Ichi remarked "I don't feel the anything coming out of my hands yet."

"Learning how to cultivate energy will take time Ichi," emphasized Grandma T. "This art form is called Chi Kung. You must use your breathing to execute the moves properly to help create both energy and strength. When you start your training at Mountain Temple, Sifu will show you more exercises to help you learn this art form."

"Aaah, that was wonderful. You are both learning well," said Grandma T. "Now, I think two hours is enough training. Let's have some lunch!"

Walking back to her home, Grandma T remarked, "I have a few more great stories to share. Then it will be time for you two to head to Iwa Village to take part in some kind of a cookout."

As they all enjoyed a scrumptious meal together, Kekoa pulled out the map as she and Ichi started to locate the route to their next location. "Look, this is where we are," pointed out Kekoa.

"Yes! Yes! You're right!" acknowledged Ichi. "Let me see here. It seems we need to follow along this really straight trail here. I've never seen a trail so straight."

"Haha! That's a fold in the map, not the trail silly," laughed Kekoa.

Ichi turned the map upside down and noticed the fold, "Oh, yeah. You're right. This is the trail," chuckled back Ichi.

"Okay. If we go along this path, we will end up at Ti Lung River. We follow the river for a few miles until we reach one of the docking stations and hitch a ride on a flatboat with Captain Goyo," added Kekoa.

The flatboat will take the kids to one of the larger villages of the area, Iwa Village. Twice a year, the farmers and fishermen donated ten percent of their goods - like food and supplies - to the village.

The townspeople would create a huge feast in front of city hall for all to enjoy and afterwards, everyone had the opportunity to stock up on food for their family for several months. It was a way for those who have benefited most to give back to the community. Every year, the monks from Mountain Temple have their new recruits assist the town by serving as chefs.

"Well, eat up you two! I have more great stories of my battles that even Sifu hasn't heard."

For the next two hours, Grandma T enjoyed sharing her adventures about being called back into the war. She didn't get many guests coming her way, so it was a delight to have the two children as company.

"Grandma T, you mean you fought in the war and then you settled down and then they called you back in," said an astonished Kekoa.

"Thirty years later young lady. Thirty years later!" added Grandma T.

"Whoa!" remarked Ichi.

"Oh yes. Haha! By then, I had me some grandchildren and everyone started calling me Grandma T. It took a dilly of a time for the military to find me, the great Tina Timora! But they found me and back to battle I went!" recalled Grandma T.

"It was like I never left, haha!" laughed Grandma T, as she slapped her knee. "Well, my young students, I've talked your ear off. So now, I think it's time for you two to get ready to continue your journey! You've still got a long road ahead of you!"

Ichi and Kekoa strapped on their packs and headed toward the door, where Grandma T was now waiting.

"Be sure to remember the lessons I taught you," commented Grandma T. "Sifu will be asking me to come to Mountain Temple a few times a year to teach you kids some more Chi Kung exercises so we'll see each other again."

"Thank you, Grandma T! We'll share these great stories with Sifu and we'll practice what you taught us," exclaimed Kekoa.

They both bowed and gave Grandma T a hug. Then, off they went into the forest to continue their journey toward Ti Lung River.

The Path Ahead

About three long hours of walking through the forest, Kekoa and Ichi decided to rest for a bit.

"Wasn't that so cool? The movements Grandma T taught us seemed so simple but it was so hard," remarked Kekoa. She then sat on the rock and pulled out Cousin Lelani's water bag.

"You were a natural, Kekoa. My balance was still a little off," confessed Ichi.

"It was my surfing that helped," noted Kekoa.

"Huh?"

"Yep. In order to surf, you have to have perfect balance or you'll fall right off the board. I've been surfing since I was two so I've had a lot of years to perfect my balance. That's what helped me," stated Kekoa. "Why don't we work on it together?"

"Thank you. I appreciate you saying that," remarked Ichi, as he got up from the rock.

For the next 20 minutes, Kekoa continued to help Ichi improve his balance and work on his breathing.

"There you go!" encouraged Kekoa. "See? I knew you could do it!"

"Thank you, Kekoa! That was kind of you," acknowledged Ichi as they sat down to rest. "Hey, you are going to enjoy meeting my cousin!"

"Shinji, right?"

"Yeah! He's more like my little brother and he's got the neatest gadgets that I know you will love! Especially his smoke bombs!" revealed Ichi.

"Wooooow! Smoke bombs! I like that!" revealed Kekoa, who then pointed toward the trees and added, "Hey, you know, if we keep going in this direction, we should hit the river pretty soon and the docking station should be nearby."

"Right! Then, let's go," said Ichi. They both got to their feet, grabbed their bags and headed in the direction of the river.

All the while, Kekoa and Ichi continued to share stories about their own personal life. Topics included their schools, their friends and - of course - homework assignments!

The afternoon was slowing coming upon them as Ichi remarked, "Kekoa, I think I hear the sound of the river."

"Yes, I hear it too."

Ichi pointed out in front of them and said, "Hey, look over there! It's the river and way over there is one of the docking stations! We made it!"

"Bet I can beat you there," challenged Kekoa, already starting to run ahead of him.

"You're on!" shouted out Ichi, as they both ran toward the docking station.

Kekoa turned around and started to run backwards. "Hey slowpoke, let's get moving!" she taunted.

"Haha! Don't wait for me!" shouted Ichi, as he ran a little faster to catch up.

Captain Goyo's Flatboat

"We beat you both!" yelled out Shinji and Lalo, as the flatboat pulled into the docking station.

"We thought you two would never get here," they laughed as Ichi stepped onto the flatboat.

"Cousin!" exclaimed Ichi, as he gave him a hug. "I think you've grown a few inches since I last saw you," as he put his hand on his head and used his own body to measure his height.

"Yeah? That was only two weeks ago," laughed Shinji.

Lalo stepped off the boat to greet Kekoa. Reaching out his hand, he said, "Hi, you must be Kekoa, it is an honor to meet you."

"And you must be Lalo," she replied. Kekoa shook his hand and gave him a hug.

"Grandma Oda has told me so much about you," Lalo revealed.

"That's right, you visited her. I hope she said only good things," Kekoa countered with a big smile.

Just then, Captain Goyo stepped off the boat onto the dock. "This is Goyo, Captain Goyo," said Shinji. "He's the owner of this vessel and he's taking us way down river to a big lake, which is where we'll find Iwa village"

"Well, welcome youngsters. Why don't you put your things in the boat while I stretch my legs out a little bit on dry shore?" said Captain Goyo, as he walked to the docking station.

"This is a great idea that Sifu had, connecting us together before we get to Mountain Temple," remarked Kekoa.

"Hey, guess who we met! You are never going to believe this. The great warrior herself, Tina Timura," revealed Ichi.

"No way!" yelled out Shinji as he turned his head in amazement. "I can't believe it!"

With a look of confusion on his face, Lalo asked, "Who's Tina Timura?"

"Who's Tina Timura!?" said all three of his fellow adventurers in unison.

Just then, Shinji put his arm around Lalo and said with a smile and waving his hand to the sky, "Well my good fellow, stick with us. We have got some amazing stories to tell you and by the time this trip is over, we are going to fill your brain with so many stories, it's going to pop!"

"Ow, that sounds really exciting! Can't wait!" replied Lalo.

"According to the captain, we are going to be traveling together for a while," remarked Shinji.

"That's right young man," agreed Captain Goyo, as he walked down the dock and back into the boat.

"Well youngsters, we still got quite a ways to go! If we're lucky, we'll get there in about a couple of days. We have a lot of stops to make along the way, as we gather more supplies and food."

"Will we make it on time for the festivities?" queried Kekoa.

"Actually, we will be right on time, since we have the food and supplies, they won't start without us," smiled Captain Goyo.

"That's right," laughed Kekoa. "Haha, I didn't think about that!"

"Make yourself a comfortable spot here on my boat. You going to be spending both days and nights here as we go down river," said Captain Goyo.

Captain Goyo's boat was actually a flatboat. It was more like a rectangular, oversized raft. It's primary function was for carrying large amounts of cargo up and down the river.

The guardrail also served as a seating area that doubled as sleeping quarters that surrounded the entire vessel. There was a large, slightly slanted canopy that stretched across the entire vessel to protect the cargo from the sun and the rain. The steering was done at the back of the boat.

For the moment, only about a two dozen bags of food and supplies were on the boat. However, by the time the trip ended, it would be so full, the kids would have barely enough room to sleep.

Everyone put down their packs and found their place on the boat. Kekoa, Ichi, Lalo and Shinji spent the better part of the day talking about meeting Tina Timura and the adventures they encountered on their journey.

Throughout the next two days, Captain Goyo made several stops on their odyssey to pick up food and supplies. Sometimes the food was ready for them at one of the docking stations, sometimes they had to go to the farms and small villages with a cart to retrieve the supplies.

Fireflies Light the Way

To make things easier for Captain Goyo, Ichi and Kekoa took turns steering the boat down river. Steering the boat was not an easy task and it took the two strongest to handle it.

The river continued to twist and turn, but with a soft calmness - like a slow-moving sloth!

At night, lanterns were hung on the four corners of the boat and the light of the moon reflected across the river to help light the way. They continued to travel late into the evening as fireflies lit up the sides of the river to help guide their path.

Through most of the late night journey, Lalo, Shinji and Captain Goyo were all sound asleep. Even though you could hear the awesome sounds of the water as it gently flowed down river, the ribbits of the frogs and the chirps of the crickets, their loud snores overpowered them all.

"Hey, Ichi," Kekoa said softly, as they maneuvered the boat together, "I'm so excited about studying at Mountain Temple. My Grandma Oda told me of the wonderful adventures she had as a young girl there."

"I know! I can hardly wait!" whispered back Ichi,

as he took over the steering from Kekoa, who sat down to rest a bit. "They say Sifu is one of the best monks to learn from. I heard he's an expert in many of the martial arts, but I'm still a little worried."

"You and me both!" exclaimed Kekoa. "It's exciting but I'm a little worried about being away from everyone back home. You're lucky, you've got your cousin to hang with! But I don't know anyone there," admitted Kekoa.

"Well....Now you know me! In time, I hope you will consider me as a brother you can lean on," sincerely noted Ichi.

Kekoa smiled and pointed out past the left side of the boat. "Oh look!" As fish just jumped out of the water and made a big splash!

It was around three in the morning when Captain Goyo woke up and wiped his eyes for a bit as he scratched under his armpits.

"Let me see here. Oh yes, you know I was sleeping so soundly that I almost forgot we were traveling downriver" said Captain Goyo. "From the looks of the stars, it must be close to three already."

Captain Goyo got up, folded up his blanket and grabbed his pillow and put them into a small cabinet and walked over to a tired-looking Kekoa and Ichi.

"It's about time you two got some rest!" he pointed out.

"I can't argue with that," Kekoa said, as they turned over the steering to Captain Goyo, as they made their way to the sleeping area they had already made for themselves.

"Goodnight Captain Goyo," Kekoa uttered as she laid her head down on her pillow.

"Goodnight Captain Goyo, goodnight Kekoa," said Ichi.

"Night brother."

After only a five minutes, Kekoa snored so loud that it was even louder than Lalo, Shinji, and Captain Goyo combined.

Over the next couple of days, Captain Goyo made over two dozen stops to pick up more supplies, as the kids put them on the flatboat. "I hope we get there soon, it's getting a little crowded here," said Shinji, as he and Lalo rolled a barrel of fresh goods on the boat.

Arriving at Iwa Village

In time, the river started to grow wider and wider and just as they turned the bend, it formed into a huge and magnificent lake. It was so big, it looked just like a miniature ocean.

"Hey you sleepy heads, we have just entered Masongsong Lake and that there way over yonder is Iwa Village," pointed out Captain Goyo, as he steered the flatboat toward the village.

"Huh? What? Iwa Village?" muttered Lalo, with his eyes still closed.

"Yessirree, your destination is just ahead," noted Captain Goyo. "The current is a little slow today and we ain't the fastest ship in the fleet, so it may take about two hours to get there."

"Yawn," came out of the mouth of Ichi as he stretched his arms far apart.

"Five more minutes," said Shinji as he turned his body to the other side and fell back asleep."

"Me, too! Five more minutes," said Lalo as they both rested their heads on their pillows.

Just then, Kekoa got up, wiped her eyes and started to look around in a haze. "Wow! There are some real waves out here, it feels like we are out on the ocean. Where did you say we are?

"Masongsong Lake. And about two hours off, is Iwa Village," said Captain Goyo.

Ichi reached into his backpack and took out his map and unfolded it as he and Kekoa looked at it closely. "Ah, let's take a look to see what our next step is."

"There! There's Iwa Village," pointed out Kekoa, "It says we're supposed to drop off our gear at the Fujioka Inn and then head to city hall. From there, they will help us get started with the cookout as we prepare serving both lunch and dinner."

"So, Chef Kekoa! This is going to be a fun experience!" said Ichi.

"I just hope we don't burn anything!"

"Hey you two sleepy heads! We are almost at Iwa Village," said Ichi to Lalo and Shinji.

"Is it five minutes already?" queried Shinji.

"We let you two sleep for an extra hour and a half," Kekoa informed them gleefully.

As Lalo and Shinji finally got up and finished putting their pillows and blankets back into their backpacks, the raft gently pulled up to the dock.

"Captain Goyo, we all thank you for bringing us here to Iwa Village," all four of the quest seekers said in unison, bowing to him with great respect.

"It was my pleasure and I expect you youngsters to cook up some good vittles, I plan to be there for lunch myself," said Captain Goyo, as the workers at the dock began to unload the bags of food and supplies from the raft as the children made their way to the Inn.

The Chefs

It was around ten in the morning when the kids dropped off of their backpacks at the Fujioka Inn and cleaned up and headed toward the food serving area in front of city hall.

"Hey, give me a minute. I need to drop off a letter to my parents at the mail station. I told them I would write. They tend to worry about me," said Lalo as pulled out a letter from his pocket that was ready to mail.

"Great idea! Let's all take a few moments to send a letter back home to let them know how we're getting along," added Ichi.

For the next fifteen minutes, the children wrote out a few short letters and handed them off at the mail station for delivery.

"Hey, there's a lot of benches over there and look, there are some people out there preparing the food to be cooked. That must be in the right place," commented Shinji.

"Right you are cousin," replied back Ichi.

There was a large, temporary eating area erected directly in front of city hall. There were approximately 40 tables set up with several large, beige canopies that provided shade for everyone.

As they got closer to the serving area, a lady with in a white apron with flour sprinkled all over her arms, legs and especially in her hair, approached the kids. "Ah, you're here. Fantastic! My name is Chef Ogawa. You may call me, Chef Ogawa."

She was holding a number of white aprons and handed them out to the group. "Here you go, one size fits all," said Chef Ogawa.

Of course, all the aprons were made for adults so they were all much too big. They actually looked like long, white dresses on their little bodies.

"There, you look great! Just fantastic!" she added.

Lalo looked over to Kekoa with an odd smile because they both looked so silly in their oversized aprons. Just then, all of them started laughing at each other.

"Okay kids. I've been doing this for about ten years already and I got it down to a science. I've created assembly-line cooking and I think it may one day catch on. Frankly, I don't know how they got along without me," revealed Chef Ogawa.

When I came along, everything was a mess. The food preparation was slow and by the time the guests got their food, it was almost cold," exclaimed Chef Ogawa with her hands on her hips. "I put my new method in motion and it works splendidly. If we all work together as a team, everything will be fine. I call my new method, 'the assembly-line', catchy, huh?"

"Now, this is your station. One of you will grab the food from the different barrels and all the bags over here. Another one of you will be assigned to actually cut the food. The next person will start putting everything on the grill and the last person will turn it over. When it's ready, pass it on to the server. Easy peasy, we don't add cheesy! Haha! I made that one up myself," laughed Chef Ogawa.

Chef Ogawa was a very funny lady. She was very thin and very tall and she was extremely organized and knew just how to make things work. Through her team-work approach and her assembly line methodology, she was able to serve the masses in a more structured fashion.

"So, young lads! Think you got the idea?" challenged Chef Ogawa who happened to be eating a carrot stick at the time.

"I think we are ready," replied back Kekoa, as she adjusted her apron to make it fit more comfortably.

"Ready!" yelled out Lalo, Shinji and Ichi in unison.

"Very good then. This is going to be wonderful! Did I tell you that you kids look great?" pointed out Chef Ogawa. "Well, I can see the villagers are heading this way."

"Okay, everyone! Let's pick a station," remarked Ichi as the noise from the hungry crowd was getting closer!

"I'll get the food from each of the barrels and bags and put them on the cutting table," commented Lalo.

"Leave the cutting to me," said Ichi, as he pulled out a couple of sharp knives from under the counter!

"Put me down for the first grill," shouted out Shinji.

"The second grill is mine then. I'll turn it over when it's ready and hand it off to the server," added Kekoa. "We can switch if anyone gets tired. We've got a lot of mouths to feed!"

"Sounds great!" exclaimed Lalo.

"Ready or not, here they come with hungry bellies! I'll line them up and then they're all yours," said Chef Ogawa, "So, let's start cookin'! Ow, I like the sound of that, 'Let's start cookin'!'"

As the masses of excited and hungry townspeople arrived, the kids followed Chef Ogawa's assembly line strategy as everyone was being served.

Re-Assembling the Assembly Line

After about thirty minutes into feeding the villagers, Shinji asked, "Hey, Ichi!"

"What do you think about adding our own special touch to this?"

"You mean doing some fine slicing and dicing and tossing and turning? replied back Ichi, as he was cutting up one of the meals.

With a pair of tongs in her hand, Kekoa added, "Yeah, this process works, but it's a little slow."

"Okay team......let's see what we can do?" replied Lalo.

As the next group of guests arrived, Lalo grabbed an ear of corn in one hand and tossed it up into the air toward Ichi, while shouting, "Here you go, brother!"

Before the food hit the table, Ichi took one of the chef's longer blades and sliced the corn in two pieces! In midair! Swish!!!!

Lalo threw a piece of chicken toward Ichi and again, he sliced it in two. With a quick move, Ichi shuffled the food across the table.

From there, Shinji grabbed it with his tongs, turned in a circle and put it on the grill. "Ssszz!" was the sound of the food cooking on the nice, hot surface.

After about a couple of minutes, Shinji threw the food up into the air. Then, Kekoa grabbed it, turned it over and put it on her side of the grill. "Nice move!" Shinji complimented Kekoa.

After a couple of minutes, Kekoa flipped the food onto a nearby plate and handed it over to the server. "There you go, kiddo!" said Kekoa.

This was the first time the entire group had worked together as a team.

"So, let's see how you kids are doing here," said Chef Ogawa, as she came by to check on her workers. Standing there for about five minutes, with the same carrot stick in her mouth and her hands on her hips watching them in action.

"Ah ha! Flipping and slicing in mid-air! Dicing and more slicing! Turning and cooking! Hmmm...." she said with her arms now crossed.

"You see! You see!" with her arms now outstretched. "I told you my method works brilliantly! Keep up the good work, team!"

"My students!" she yelled out in gratitude and acknowledgement to everyone in line.

The kids cooked all day, from lunch to dinner! By the end of the day, they were exhausted!

"Boy, that was fun but it was a lot of work! I'm so bushed," said a very tired Shinji as he sat down, drinking a cup of water.

"Me too! Whoever thought cooking would wear you out," joked Lalo.

"I've never cut so much food in my life! My hands feel like lead," laughed Kekoa. "Let's head over to the Inn and get a good nights' rest, I think we earned it!"

"You said it!" said Ichi. "Hey, it's starting to get a little chilly out here and the wind is starting to kick up a bit. I will welcome a nice, warm bed."

"Hey, I think I felt a drop of rain?" remarked Lalo, as he held his hands out to catch a few drops.

The kids made their way to the Fujioka Inn, which was just down the road from city hall. The moment they reached inside the doorway, the rains began. "Whew!" exclaimed Shinji, "I guess we made it just in time!"

The winds continued to blow and the rain started to come down a bit harder.

A Stormy Catastrophe

A couple of hours later, the winds continued to grow and became even stronger! Flashes of lighting appeared across the sky as the rumble of thunder awakened the ground.

Just then, a bolt of lightning struck so close to the Inn that it woke up Shinji from a sound sleep!

Shinji rushed toward the window and saw the wind blowing like a hurricane!

He noticed that several of the canopies from the food area had become loose and were flapping in the wind. The bell started to ring ferociously as the bell tower structure began to wobble back and forth!

Shinji ran over to Ichi and shook him a bit while saying, "Cousin! I think we have a problem! The rain is really coming down strong and the winds are getting pretty bad out there! It's starting to damage the village!"

Ichi joined Shinji as they looked out the window together. "Whoa, this is not good!" deduced Ichi. "Let's wake everyone!"

Shinji ran down the hallway yelling for Kekoa and Lalo to wake up, knocking feverishly on their doors.

"Wake up! The village needs our help!"

"Hey, what's up Shinji," asked Kekoa, as she followed him into Ichi's room. Just then, another lighting bolt struck the ground and it felt like an earthquake!

Kekoa quickly rushed to the window as Lalo joined her.

Shinji began to put on his coat and headed toward the door as Kekoa called out, "Let's not just rush out there! Let's plan this out!"

"What do you have in mind?" asked Shinji.

"Ichi, we need a bunch of wooden stakes to put into the ground to hold those canopies down, so we'll need your cutting skills," pointed out Kekoa.

"Lalo, if you can find some extra rope, your lassoing skills will come in handy here to help tie things down."

"Right," nodded Lalo.

"Shinji, since you are the fastest, you start knocking on the doors of the villagers! Get all the help we can," Kekoa added.

"I'll work on the bell tower and secure it before it falls down," commented Kekoa, "Just like we served the food as a team, let's help this village as a team."

The kids ran into action and in moments, the whole town became involved!

The townsfolk gathered clubs and hammers to tie

down the canopies and to secure anything that had become loose. Ropes were also used to secure the bell tower and small sandbags were placed in front of every door to prevent the rain from coming in.

Although most of the food was still safely covered with tarps, Kekoa and Shinji didn't want to push their luck.

So, they had the villagers form a long assembly line to gather the food and store it in a much dryer place.

The storm continued late into the night as Shinji, Lalo, Ichi and Kekoa worked together with the residents to secure the town and save the food.

It wasn't until another three hours, until everything was fastened down, that the kids finally got back to sleep!

The Journey Ahead

The next morning the rain storm had subsided as the children woke up to a bright and sunny day. It was time to once again to begin their trek to Mountain Temple!

"Wow, that was one really big storm! But it looks like everything is safe and secure," said Ichi, as he looked out the window as everyone started to gather into Ichi's room to prepare for their journey.

"That was a lot of work, but I think we really work well together," declared Kekoa.

"Good thing I brought a few extra pairs of shoes, mine are still soaked," joked Shinji, as he held them up to dry.

Lalo reached into his backpack, "Oh Kekoa! I forgot! Grandma Oda wanted me to give you this," recalled Lalo, as he handed her a bracelet.

"My bracelet! I forgot it! Thank you so much for bringing it," exclaimed Kekoa, as she put the bracelet on her left wrist. "Even though it's only been about five days, I miss Grandma Oda already!"

"Did you know that Grandma Oda even taught me how to surf," Lalo happily recalled, as he secured the straps on his backpack.

"No way! That's so cool! Grandma Oda is the best surfer ever. She taught me how to surf as well," said Kekoa.

As Kekoa looked down at her bracelet, she remembered that she also had something special. "That reminds me.... Hey, Ichi," remarked Kekoa, as she reached into her bag.

"What's up?" replied Ichi as he was putting a few things in his backpack.

"I have a welcoming gift for you! I should have given it to you earlier but with everything going on, I forgot!" Kekoa confessed, as she pulled out a bag of peanuts.

"Peanuts!" shouted out Ichi. "How did you know?"

"Your love for peanuts is legendary, dear brother! Here you go," as she tossed him the bag of nuts into the air!

Ichi caught the bag in one hand and, with a slight bow, he said, "Thank you, Kekoa! I am honored."

"You can't say this journey hasn't be exciting!" laughed Shinji. "We still have another full day and a half until we get there," as they headed toward the door.

Turning back to speak to Lalo, Shinji said, "I heard there were a thousand steps to climb when we reach the bottom of the Temple!"

"Really? Is that true?" remarked a surprised Lalo.

"That's what I heard! Isn't that true Ichi," asked Shinji.

"Well, I know there are a lot of steps but I really don't think there are that many," answered Ichi," as he pulled out his map.

The four of them looked at the map together. "It looks like we go in this direction and in about three hours, we hit this little eating place where we can have lunch," said Kekoa.

"Lunch! Wohoo!" exclaimed Lalo and Shinji.

"I'm getting the feeling that you two really enjoy your meals," smiled Kekoa.

Since Sifu arranged for Lalo to visit Kekoa's home village, the two of them were able to talk for hours about the Ohana Festival and the ancestry shells of her family tree.

That evening was going to be a special time for them, because it was the eve of a new page in their life. It was an adventure that they would all share together and it would have an impact on the rest of their lives.

Just then, the pathway opened up into a prepared camping area. Ichi said, "I believe this is the place we are supposed to camp tonight."

"Oh, look, there are four hammocks!" exclaimed Lalo, as he and Shinji tried to outrun each other and claim one as their own!

Kekoa remarked, as she hung her backpack on the tree, "This is a very nice campground. Look, there's a big fire pit right in the center. Let's get some sticks and we'll make a lovely fire for the evening."

"Hey, I've got some marshmallows in my backpack that I got from Captain Goyo!" said Lalo, as his stomach began to growl.

"Nice going Lalo! Let's get a couple of thin, long sticks and start some cooking!" exclaimed Shinji.

That evening, they all sat around the campfire and ate their dinner! Then, they topped it off by roasting Captain Goyo's marshmallows!

"Lalo," Kekoa said, as she turned to face him, "I've talked your ear off about my village! Let's talk about yours and Ichi's and Shinji's home. I've been to each of your villages before, but never stayed long enough to learn about them."

"However!" exclaimed Kekoa, as she raised her hand, as if to answer a question at school. "But before we begin sharing," as she looked at Shinji, "you have to demonstrate those smoke bombs everyone keeps talking about!"

"Haha! I thought you'd never ask!" Shinji smiled and laughed so hard, he fell back in his seat!

Shinji sprinted to his backpack and grabbed a handful of smoke bombs. He passed them out to everyone and said, "This is how it's done, kiddos!" as he threw his on the ground."

Everyone had a great time igniting their smoke bombs and in just moments, the entire campground was filled with smoke.

Reaching Mountain Temple

The following day the children traveled for another six hours through the forest. Stopping now and then for breakfast and lunch and to rest up a bit, they finally reached the bottom of Fu Sheng Mountain.

"Look, here it is! Fu Sheng Mountain!" exclaimed Shinji as he jumped in the air and stomped on the first of many steps. "We made it!"

"Wow, this is amazing!" said Lalo, as he looked at the steps seeing how far they went up. He leaned so far back, he actually fell backwards as Shinji caught him!

"Thanks, Shinji," Lalo said, as they laughed together.

"I can't believe we made it!" said Ichi, with a big grin with his hands on his waist, "Are we ready?"

Kekoa looked at everyone and said, "Let's wait here for just a bit, I want to soak in this moment."

After about five minutes, Shinji nudged Lalo and said, "How about you and me race to the top?"

"Usually I would take you up on that offer. But, I think we should do this together! Step by step! As a team!" explained Lalo.

"You're right! We are a team," said Shinji.

"We are family!" declared Kekoa.

"Yes we are!" said Ichi as they each hugged each other.

Off they went, step by step, as they soaked in their surroundings. Taking their time, it took about 10 minutes to reach that last step onto Mountain Temple.

They could see Sifu at the doorway of the temple, anxiously awaiting their arrival.

Together, with a look of awe in their face, they walked toward Sifu. About ten feet away, they took off their backpacks, got down on their knees and bowed to Sifu to show their respect.

"Sifu, we are honored to be here," they all said in unison.

Sifu brushed his beard with one hand, smiled at the children and said, "Welcome home young children! Welcome home."

And so, the adventure had begun....

Index of Characters, Events and Locations

Nation:
Siulum

Primary Villages:
Tomi Village
Kawa Village
Waimea Village
Meiyo Kingdom

Special Locations:
Mountain Temple
Fu Sheng Mountain
Ti Lung River
Nabe River
Masongsong Lake
Dragon Inn
Fujioka Inn
Chiba Restaurant
Fang Shi Yu Restaurant
Mulan Inn

Smaller Villages:
Shang Na Village
Keena Village
Iwa Village

Celebrations:
Festival of Life
Ohana Festival

Special Items:
The Great Tree

Unique Characters
Grandma T/Tina Timura
  Great Warrior
Captain Goyo
  Flatboat Captain
Manu
  Boyhood friend
  of Grandma Oda
Noemi
  Wife of Manu
Sensei Kubota
  School Teacher
Chef Ogawa
  Head Chef
Araki Maru
  Stage Driver
Louie Sato
  Homeowner
Travelers
  Masao, Mamiko, Michie,
  Sara, Goyo (grandkids)
Mayor Abesamis
Museum Curator
  Mr. Matsuda
The Deli-man
The Storekeeper

Ichi

11 years old
Lives in Tomi Village
Toshi, Father
Rumiko, Mother
Fumio, Uncle
  (Brother of Toshi)
Takemi, Aunt
  (Childhood friend of Rumiko)
Shinji, Cousin
Ishii, Great Aunt

Kekoa

10 years old
Lives in Waimea Village
Kimo, Father
Waiola, Mother
Kiwani Oda, Grandma Oda
Kaihewalu Oda, Grandpa
Tichia Nava, Great Grandma
Makuota "Maku the Mighty"
  Great Grandpa
Lelani, Cousin

Shinji

9 years old
Lives in Kawa Village
Fumio, Father
Takemi, Mother
Toshi, Uncle
  (Brother of Fumio)
Rumiko, Aunt
  (Childhood friend of Takemi)
Ichi, Cousin

Lalo

9 years old
Lives in the Kingdom of Meiyo
Prince Zafu, Father
Princess Cynthia, Mother
King Fari Roiles, Grandfather
Queen Lori Roiles,
  Grandmother
Thora, Head Servant
Gene Roiles,
  Great Grandfather
Prado Roiles,
  Great Great Grandfather

Sifu

Age unknown
Lives at Mountain Temple
Last Name: Kong
Sister: Rola
  (not mentioned)

Questions for Thought

1. Ichi could have enrolled at Mountain Temple earlier, why did he wait?

2. How is Shinji related to Ichi?

3. What do the sea shells represent?

4. Which persons share a connnection with Grandma Oda?

5. Why did Ichi's father tell him to explore acting, singing, drawing, etc.?

6. Which skill did Grandma Oda teach to Lalo?

7. Why was it important Lalo spend time at Kekoa's village?

8. Family history is mentioned in two villages. Which are they?

9. The are two terms for teacher. Which are they?

10. There are two mighty warriors mentioned. Who are they?

11. Grandma Oda gave Lalo and item to give to Kekoa. What was it?

12. Ichi's favorite thing to eat is what?

13. Sifu's favorite thing to drink is what?

14. Write a short eassy on what you feel is the message of the book?

Book One: The Adventures of Ichi and His Friends